Buried
Treasure

Dedication

All honor and glory to the Lord Jesus Christ, who, in the power of the Holy Spirit, risked it all, even death, for the sake of love.

In tribute to my late father Victor, a man with unshakeable honesty, real character and a great sense of humor, and Marie, a mother whose unwavering faith lived out in a remarkably unselfish life taught me that love is stronger than death, and that a promise from God, and to God, is worth it all. Song of Solomon 8:6

Contents

Chapter 1

"Tell Them I Am Coming"

20th Century Man

"Doesn't it amaze you that 20th century man
Has entered in and taken part of God's prophetic plan
Can she be brought forth in a moment, the Lord inspired
Isaiah to say
Israel lives to testify a country was born in a day.

Daniel's oracle tells us that the days are not so far away
that men will rise from their graves
some to everlasting glory, others to a damnable shame.

The living Messiah told us all we ever need to know
He said it would be like Noah's day
seed is planted, fruit still grows
so what is your decision people of this time
the grape is ripe for harvest, the fruit is off the vine.

Summer, winter, spring or fall
man rides the pages of them all
Time is made for men to choose holy lives or none at all
Two women stood side by side
I turned for a moment
the other was gone.

The earth is ripe, the earth is full
She is pregnant with the season of her Lord
Deliver to us, O Zion, a morning child.

The whole earth cries out a labor pain,
a push, a pull she cannot understand
something strange and wonderful is about to begin
Hail the King! That Awaited name! The Lamb's Book of Life
will your name be entered in?

And here's a secret for 20th century man
I hear you like a mystery, now hear my Father's plan:
"Not all of us will be asleep
the day the trump doth sound"
Quicker than a camera's flash
I will be glory-bound."

Elizabeth Mickel
© 1985

God's Summer Plans for 1994 A Trip to the Middle East

It was August of 1990, and I remember waking in the middle of the night. I heard the voice of the Lord clearly saying to me, "Jeremiah 50 and 51." When the Good Shepherd speaks, His sheep hear His voice. As I read those living words, I knew that this was a word for this hour of time. In the next few weeks, as the Gulf War blew open, I remembered His words, and thought often about the Middle East, Israel, America, as well as my own life and what God was saying to me. The Word of God says "here a little, there a little, line upon line, precept upon precept" because God builds us in truth as we walk out His Living Word.

About two years later, a friend sent me a tape in the mail from a preacher who was knowledgeable about eschatology (end-time events). As I listened to the pastor's lucid teaching about the countries in the Middle East and how God's Word illuminates the times we live in, [especially when reference was made to Babylon (particularly verse 33 of Jeremiah 50)], I understood the dreams and words the Lord had given me more clearly than I had in five years. This pastor was quoting the same chapters that were underlined in my Bible, for the Spirit of God kept prompting me to read Zechariah 12 and Jeremiah 50, 51.

Isaiah 11:11 speaks of gathering the remnant for a second time in history. For over 10 years the Lord had been speaking to me about "gathering the remnant, the second time" and within an instant, the Lord flooded my memory with His Words, all the prophecies, all the things He had said. This is how the disciples must have felt when they went with the resurrected Jesus on that famous "Emmaus walk." "Did not our heart burn within us," they said (see Lk. 24:32).

When the Spirit of God bears witness and confirms His Word, the truth of it is that the presence of God just quickens us. Lovers call it "a look," scientists call it an illumination, believers know the fragrance of His presence. He just confirms it when it is of Him, **"This is the way, walk ye in it."**

The God of Abraham, Isaac and Jacob is about to do another Old Testament miracle in New Testament time. His Word is like lightning that flashes in the sky (see Mt. 24:27, 28:3). The God of Revelation imparts light. From 1991 to 1993 there were countless times I would recall the dream I had in 1983 of the Lord piercing the eastern sky, of the Lion of Judah riding a white horse, leading an army of saints coming with power, might, and glory, dressed as He is described in the Books of Daniel, Joel, and Revelation. I do not possess the language to describe the glory or fear of God that I felt for that instant, but I think I know how John, who wrote the Book of Revelation, must have felt as he said, "I fell at His feet as a dead man." No flesh can stand before the Son of God in all His glory. It is essential we stand dressed in the garment of His salvation, washed by His blood, or we cannot stand at all.

In the Old Testament, Jeremiah chapters 49 through 51 speaks of the harvest that is to come (see Jer. 51:33). The nation of Israel will fight again, as she did in times past, and let the nations around her know, "This border (Gaza Strip) was my inheritance, not from man, but God." God promised a deed of land generations ago, and that deed was not forgotten. Not when the nation was scattered abroad because of their disobedience to God, not even when they were only a few. Even after the Holocaust, when God brought them back to their land, no one, no one, could uproot them. Remember the six-day war? How could one tiny land win with so great an army against it? The same way King David and his army defeated their foes who outnumbered them: when God's land is the prize, He will send even angels to fight and march around the walls.

Bethlehem is the city of the Great King, and the Lord Himself will one day stand on the Mount of Olives again. God has an eternal inheritance in *that* city, and He will see to it that Israel is never again without their home. Understand, God loves all men, He doesn't play favorites, and His Word is certain. He gave a gift to men of faith such as Abraham and Moses, for their seed forever, and He will not have any man taking what belongs to Him. Would you like a scud missile aimed at you saying, "Give me your house that has been in your family for thousands of years, the land where your ancestors paid by blood to sacrifice and pray it into destiny"? I think not.

In the 1980s the Lord would often speak to me about "*70 years*," and I believe He is now completing and restoring all things. After the second gathering of God's people to their land in 1948, God's Word says He will fight for Israel, when the harvest is full, or when the time is ripe. Read Jeremiah chapters 49, 50 and 51; it is happening now. Ancient Philistia, the Gaza Strip, even the nations of Jordan (Ammon), Damascus, modern-day Syria, even Egypt and Iraq are there. The old Babylonian empire is still around, just with different names. And the fight between Isaac and Ishmael, the two sons of Abraham, is still re-enacted in the land today.

Just as Abraham had to send Ishmael out to find his own land, God declared prophetically that the fruit of his seed, Isaac, was to inherit the land. Do not doubt God's love for Ishmael (Arab nations), as well as Isaac (Israel's seed). God loves the seed of Ishmael as one of His sons. Abraham was a prototype of our Father offering His Son, His only Son, on the altar. Just as our Heavenly Father sent Jesus as a sin offering, Abraham was willing to obey God to the point of laying down what meant most to Him: His Son. Yet God was not after the blood of Abraham's child; He was testing Abraham's obedience, and we know he passed the test.

Isaac was born to Abraham and Sarah miraculously in their very old age, as a witness, to the power of God. God always has a vested interest in a miracle: it is a living witness to the glory of His Son. God wanted to and still does bless Ishmael; yet God has a plan and purpose under heaven for every child and nation. Ishmael couldn't be an Isaac; he had his own destiny in God. This is what the war in the Middle East is really about: destiny. The Jews' very existence proves the only true religion is that of the God of the Ten Commandments. The God of Moses is still alive today. All (believing!) Christians today have been grafted into the vine, who is

Jesus, by the first Jews—from Abraham to Paul and the disciples—who bore witness to the Messiah. We owe a great deal to the lineage of Jesus Christ.

The words of Zephaniah, chapter 2, and Zechariah 12:2 reveal that God will cause Jerusalem to be "a cup of trembling to all the people round about." Jeremiah 49:24 declares that the oldest city on earth will become a "ruinous heap." God prophetically declares what the relationship will be between Israel and her neighbors on all her borders. It is not God's will (read Ezekiel chapter 38) to give the West Bank (the Gaza Strip) to anyone other than whom it was deeded to 6,000 years ago: Abraham and his posterity. The only piece of real estate in this earth that God called His wife, that was deeded to Abraham, that wars would be fought in, (a cup of trembling the Scripture called it), is Israel. It is the city where Christ will rule and reign with justice. The nations of the earth will soon see that you cannot steal God's deeds and not go unnoticed. The nations that are after His land will soon be sifted like powder. Repentance will come after the earth realizes that it cannot play games with the Almighty's covenants and vows. Millions of tears and oceans of blood were lost for a tiny piece of real estate, and God will not have that sacrifice forgotten.

After 70 years of Babylonian captivity, God returned Israel to their land. God will wipe out in a day the plans made in secret to wipe out a nation. Zechariah 12:2 shows that Jerusalem will be made a cup of trembling. Not to say Israel won't experience very difficult times. Not to say it won't be hard (see Isaiah 17:4). Yes, there are rough days ahead for Israel (see Ezekiel 38), but God will not forsake her. Yet not until their Prince of Peace returns will there be *real* peace. Ezekiel 38 tells us that what the countries think in secret, God reveals openly. Persia (Iran and Iraq) is in the Scriptures, as well as Gomer (Germany). Togarmah (Turkey), Meshech (Moscow), and Rosh (Russia) were first penned by the prophets thousands of years ago. Ezekiel 38:2 is just one of many verses that reveal God knows the beginning and end of all things. Try reading the newspaper with God's viewpoint. It's a real eye opener. Isaiah 15:1 tells us Moab is attacked in the night; in Scripture *night* speaks of being caught unaware, and *dark* speaks of the physical night. God is practically writing today's headlines for everyone to see. Soon, on a summer night, the night-rider will turn the page for Judah's lion.

God is not a hard God. He doesn't tell us to repent without reason. Sin kills the life of God in us. How can we hear God with a stubborn heart?

How can you know Him if you don't read His letters? With the infilling of the Holy Spirit, His life interprets the words for you, as He is the author. No coach or trainer worth his salt would tell an athlete competing for the medal, "Take it easy, run less, eat more junk food, watch more TV, and forget your exercise regimen." In life, without the daily stuff, there is no gain. How much more necessary is it in matters of destiny and salvation to learn how to listen to God's voice?

"I am pregnant with the seasons, and I will give birth to a summer child."

The above words are a little tune that came to mind that I used to hum while cleaning. The Lord gave me that song years ago, and this year I know what those words really mean to Israel and the Church. This message from the Lord was buried in me for a long, long time. Some things are buried for a season because it is not needed at the time, and some treasures are buried because one doesn't know what to do with them at the time. Jesus said unless a seed falls to the ground and dies (buried in the earth), it cannot bring forth fruit (see Jn. 12:24). The only part of us that will eternally bear fruit is that which God redeems. Because the Lord is wise and full of purposeful mercy, He uses even our weakness to bring forth His strength.

As a heavy sleeper who usually needs a half pot of java to get my motor going at 6:00 a.m., when I wake up refreshed and wide awake at 3:00 a.m., I can assure you, if He wakes you (which He said He would do in the last days, according to Joel 2:28), He is not there to play checkers. Recently, the Lord awoke me with a certainty, "Read Jeremiah 49." On went the light, out came the atlas, globe and Bible, and there I sat looking at these ancient lands (Philistia, West Bank, Gaza Strip, Damascus, Syria today, Ammon and Moab, the area of Jordan). Until 4:00 a.m. I sat looking at places like Egypt, Iraq, and Iran. I poured over old articles, prophecies, newsletters and turned the highlighted and crinkled pages of Jeremiah and Isaiah. There it was, plain as day: the Middle East is about to experience (and very soon) the same kind of miraculous intervention and sovereign acts that the God of the Old Testament did, for today's Kingdom-Age times.

God blew down the walls of Jericho, and more than once, He protected Israel's borders with displays of His protection.

The Father of Jesus is about to do it again; perhaps by summer, God is going to show the nations aiming to steal what they call "occupied territory," land which was deeded by God to Abraham and all his seed, how He defends His borders. It's all there in black and white: whether it is the P.L.O. or some other adversary, God is going to fight this battle. His word declares it. You can't get to page seven in the daily news without hearing about the Gaza Strip and the war and the violence. No matter what your political persuasion or views on the trouble in the Middle East, you cannot undo anything God has prophesied.

God does not play favorites, He executes justice. God is the only true, just Judge. You weren't around 4,000 years ago when the Jews lost their homeland. You didn't see the generations of tears. You were not there when only a devil could infiltrate a man's mind so much as to produce servants of evil with the atrocities of the Holocaust. God saw it all, heard it all. Every broken bone, every smashed child, and miles of blood. Do you really think He is going to let Israel be stolen from again? Do you not think He will Himself fight the battle, as He did in the six-day war when God sent angels to blow winds so heavy that a tiny nation the size of New Jersey wiped out the armies that outnumbered her in foot soldiers and weaponry?

When God is on your side **(and He is on the side of any covenant He promises and declares)** you will be amazed. People laughed at Joshua as he walked around Jericho seven times, yet no one laughed when it took days to pick up the bricks that fell on those who mocked the God of Israel. What about ol' Elijah? No one laughed when God sent fire from heaven and made a fool of the false prophets and sorcerers. God doesn't need to prove anything; He does not display His power without reason. He loves His own, and His own are those who love the One who was sent.

The Jews made a covenant to God 4,000 years ago, and although many still wait for the Messiah to appear, there are many today who are discovering that *He* is already come, and *His* name is Jesus. Those who are curious should pick up the Old Testament; Jesus fulfilled all that was written of Him (see Daniel, Joel and Isaiah, for starters). But even a skeptic can't refute the power of His presence, and once the Holy Spirit reveals Jesus to you, no one will ever have to convince you who He is.

Like a patchwork quilt, here a little, there a little, line upon line, precept upon precept, in moments of rest and peace, the gentle dove will come to us and teach us "what no man can teach us." After a long wilderness, the Lord our God has been trying to tell us that "He is coming soon" in a way we did not expect. The Lamb grew up to become a Lion, and for those not abiding in His Life, they will not be able to endure the coming move of God. Lest anyone think God waits around every 500 years or so to whip hurricanes and tornadoes and the sounds of war to earth for a little adventure, His word tells us that He remembers that we are flesh. He restrains judgments because if He did not "no flesh would live."

He calls, travails, whispers, and pleads for us so He can show His mercy. He might speak to a man a thousand times in his lifetime of the need for salvation, but a stubborn and rebellious heart turns away. He begs nations not to murder and to turn from evil, but who really listens? No nation was ever destroyed without years and generations of pleading and warnings. The Shepherd Himself pours out so many blessings so people will "taste and see the goodness of God" and turn to Him. God even says, "Come let us reason together; though your sins be as scarlet, I'll make you white as snow." God does not want to crack open the earth to get man's attention, but when whole generations have heard in books and songs and from preachers and old grandmothers that "Jesus is coming soon," why are innocent lives still murdered, why is crime called good, and holiness called evil?

Jesus' words in Matthew 24 show us the King is serious about establishing His Kingdom, and if He can't get our attention quietly whispering to our heart, He will shout if He has to. The Son of God is soon to be glorified in all the earth. When nations see a supernatural move of God on earth, they will look up.

The trip the Israelites made through the desert many centuries ago is a lesson for us today: as the glory cloud in the wilderness was a protection, guide, and covering for the Israelites, it was sure judgment and death to those who opposed the moving and working of God's Holy Spirit. Doubt it? Hmm. Just ask the bones of Pharaoh and his troops. What would Hamon say today about his plans to kill off Esther and Mordecai? Point is folks, the hour of decision has come, and there is no turning back. Yes, this sounds like an alarm because it is. Amos cried, Hosea cried, Joel cried, and the bride of Christ cries...there is not much time yet to sign up for eternity.

It is too late when a killer tornado blows your life apart, and it is too late when you lie under the bricks of a building destroyed by an earthquake. Even in His righteous judgments, God is still full of mercy. "Miraculously," the great L.A. quake happened in the early hours on a weekend. Coincidence? Think again. While we all slept, God had dispatched armies of angels to keep millions alive and safe. He is shouting, "Wake up and come to the Maker," while there is yet time, all the while sparing the lives of millions. He shouts through blizzards, hurricanes, earthquakes, floods, train wrecks, car wrecks, cancer, war, and all manner of ills. What does God have to do to wake up the living dead?

Friends, one day this world will be set on fire. As Billy Joel's song said, "We didn't start the fire. It was always burning since the world was turning." How true. God ignited the flame. He makes His ministers, those who know Him in spirit and truth, a "living flame." When the Holy Ghost is living in you—you have the flame of eternal light that will never go out. The Lord Jesus came not for social action, but divine mediation: He became our Mediator. He did not come to "keep man's peace," but to give God's righteousness in exchange for man's sin. While He walked on earth, the sleeping church of that day wanted the healings, the blessings, the riches and the power, without repentance, a real change of heart.

Christ didn't come to make us nice; He came to make us real. Our Heavenly Father wants the personality and personhood of the Living Christ, the nature of God, to live in us. Of course God wants to heal and bless, that is the very heartbeat of a good father, and the Father of billions of souls is full of mercy. He wants to deliver us from ourselves to heal us. God wants to heal us, but it will never happen without a heart repentance.

Churches that promote and license what God calls perversion and abominations can have all the services they want—God will not show up on the scene in a place where His Word is mocked. Many heresies abound in this time we live in. Anyone who teaches that it is *not* necessary to believe on the blood of Jesus Christ for salvation is teaching a lie. It is just as necessary today to believe on the blood and resurrection of Jesus Christ as it was 2,000 years ago. Does anyone realize satan laughs and mocks and can't wait to deceive a generation to be in misery forever with him? Remember Lazarus? Jesus spoke of hell often, not to make people miserable, but to warn them because He loved them. Read Jesus' words to the churches in the Book of Revelation. The message is applicable to all who name the name of Jesus as their God.

What parent does not bundle up their precious two-year-old before going out in the cold? What parent would not feed or clothe or care for their young? If your little one insists on playing with matches and playing in the streets, the reality of a hospital visit can break your heart. And even in this sorrow, it is only a lifetime. Just as wise parents take precautions to ensure the safety of their young, our Lord has provided a Saviour to keep us from harm, and to watch us in all our steps. His blood has provided even an escape from the fires of hell.

Is not pride the worst sin? "We don't need God." We'll keep Him on our currency (and the spirit of mammon is planning on changing that soon, too) and say the obligatory God prayers at opening ceremonies and courtroom oaths, but don't you tell me what to do with my life, my body, my choices. Blood of multiple millions has cried to God. What shall God do? How shall He answer these little ones? You think this is a rhyme? God told Cain that Abel's blood cried out to Him. Science, centuries later, is finally catching on that God's Word is alive. Scientists are now discovering our bodies have noises and our souls have a voice of their own. The first half of the 20th century coupled the findings of the academic and scientific world, giving credibility to what believers have known all along: God's Word is true. When scientists, archaeologists, and explorers discover what they believe to be remnants of Noah's Ark, or fragments of the Dead Sea scrolls, God is unveiling history at His prophetic timing. With one strong right arm, God dismantled communism's walls in a "prophetic" hour. If you are baptized in the Holy Spirit and know His voice, He makes His Word alive to you. He teaches you history "before it ever happens."

God is no respecter of persons. His invitation for new life and the presence of Jesus within is open to "all who come." When a nation listens and repents, that nation will have as its Judge, Lawyer, Soldier, Friend, Financier and Benefactor the Living God, for He promises to bless without measure those who listen and observe His words (Deuteronomy 28), and to deal with the nations that do not.

God tells us clearly what He will not do. He will not lay down with a harlot. He chose poor old Hosea to marry a harlot to speak to Israel, and the Church, all the gentile nations, came from her. Don't forget that all God's dealings with Israel apply as clearly to the Church today as to them because Jesus is the New Covenant, which fulfilled the old. When you walk in faith and trust with God, He will show you Himself. And **in Him** is the beginning and end of all things.

He blows through America at 90 miles an hour; He crushes our highways with the breath of His nostrils, and yet, "the summer is ended, the harvest is over, and we are all not yet saved."

America, we need to wake up before a blast comes out of the mouth of God. Don't ever think God is not in control: even satan is only a rabid dog on a leash, and one day soon, God will end that mad dog's life forever. God has final authority in all things; He just uses things, people, and spirits to chastise and correct when absolutely necessary to save us. When Israel obeyed God, God brought His glory so strong on that nation, that even "heathen" nations feared the God of Israel. When nations get careless and forget and mock their God with idols, He allows strong nations to overtake and oppress them. When a single soul or a nation obeys God, He will turn the earth around to bless. But He cannot bless sin.

There is not enough money in Congress to heal our ills, and there isn't enough vaccine in America to heal our wounds. Now you know why the prophet spoke of an incurable wound. God will deliver the nation that falls on its knees and wets its face with tears when it repents and really means it. Like a mate who has an unfaithful spouse only to be caught, confess contrition, then sneak out and take on more lovers, God has blessed us so fat we had no lack. But America has too many lovers. The Son of God will not visit a church that condones sin, and He will not visit with mercy those who oppress the poor. He will not bless the courtroom with true justice when bribes count more than truth, and He will not deliver America from the big bomb which is even now aimed at us when we throw blood before His face all day long.

It is next to a national shame to call things what they *truly* are today. Orwell was right: we have become a nation of doublespeak. People were saved from the clutches of hell because the Messiah and those like Him ("whoever does my Father's will is My mother and brother...") wanted to please God more than please man. Isn't it plain why Jesus said "you can't please man and God"?

If we want a future, we have to remember that it was prayer, and most of all God's choice, that established us as a nation. If we want to live, if you want your children to live, we have to teach them something more important than even their own names: we have to teach them about Jesus, about the love of God, and about the salvation He offers. There will be no more free rides on God's boat, the gravy train is over. Within the next few years, major disasters, far greater than the weather channel has shown us the last few years, will nearly bury this land. Is this gloom-and-doom or is it a reason to rejoice? It is simply the truth: God loves us and wants to restore our nation and our souls, but we must be willing to change. All of us.

What if famine were to wipe us out? Fear and hopelessness would be the diet of the day. What a set-up for the antichrist government prophesied so long ago. Uncle Sam is not our breadbasket; he was just a lion's cub that God showed great mercy to so that He could reach many nations by His right hand.

God says in His Word that He does nothing without first revealing it to His servants. No one who lives in this nation can truly say, "I didn't know about Christ." Books have been written, movies have been made, calamity after calamity has heralded the King's soon return. Whether it's TV or the church around the corner or that wonderful presence you knew was God when you said your prayers last night, we can't truly say, "God, I never heard the words 'get ready,' I never heard about Your return." Who in America has not known of or heard some prophet, evangelist, priest, or teacher say, "Prepare to meet thy Maker"? We all have heard, and we are responsible to hear and obey God, one on one.

God will cause the nations to listen and stop dead in their tracks in a moment of time. Why? Because God gave the West Bank to Israel, period. He sets up and raises low. Because the same God who turned Babylon upside down in one day and tore Europe apart in an hour of time has plans and purposes for nations. His utmost purpose is that all men be saved: Jew, Hindu, Moslem, atheist, even Christians in name only who have yet to become it in heart, all are fruit for His harvest.

Truth is, the spirit of Cain, who killed his brother Abel, and of Ishmael, who hated his brother Isaac, is alive today:

even nations are jealous. God doesn't fight a war just to say one side is all good and the others are all evil. No nation was punished as hard for her sins as the nation that knows God but turns her back on Him. Has Israel's destiny foreshadowed an ominous destiny for the land of the eagle: America? When God has made us fat with blessings and the envy of the nations (see Deut. 28) due to the oaths and covenants made with God, we cannot risk presumption at thinking our (America's) punishment will not be as severe as the nation that God *first* swore to. The words of our Constitution and Declaration of Independence directly state we have set the Living God as our seal and our oath. We were once committed to God, and did not shrink back from our faith. Our survival depends on allegiance to the God who formed our isles of freedom's shores.

How can a nation that wants God's name on their money and working overtime to keep the weather good, crops growing, storms at sea, and our borders safe, then, turn around and curse Him, blaspheme Him in parades, mock Him in the courtroom by not fearing to take false oaths, and take Him out of our schools and public institutions by making it illegal to pray?

I don't care if the A.C.L.U. thinks you can take God out of the books, I know the God who opens them on the last day when you stand before Him (see Rev. 20:11-15). I tell you, one visit from the Lord in His glory would make any unbeliever quickly repent. And when you repent, you don't work against His Kingdom, you serve it.

I wonder if our society thinks that God is some old fuddy-duddy who will just sit there, generation after generation, and be insulted? Movies are made that desecrate His name, banners are seen in parades that call God gay, and "doctrines of devils" teach little ones in schools that they can be God. Children are given condoms instead of life; they are not taught respect for themselves, that they are holy and precious and a living soul. When their music tells them about death, how can they know of life? Why are irresponsible musicians and a media concerned more with money than morés allowed to get away with it? It is because they want man's approval and this earth's mammon more than what is right. People even make a pact with the devil for fame. What a sorry way to meet one's Maker; what a legacy to carry over into eternity.

Yet, God is working in our midst. His glory and holiness is about to be revealed. "Prepare ye the way of the Lord." He is about to visit this generation, this time called "The Kingdom of God."

And in all this, with sins piled high to heaven, His deepest desire is to still save us, forgive us, cleanse us…so we could have a new life, a new nation, and our names written in Heaven's rollbooks. What more could He do?

p.s.: In case you wondered how we got in such a sore state, it is called sin. God is cleaning house. When Jesus rules and reigns (the Kingdom Age), it will be what He intended it to be before sin messed up the whole planet, back in that garden.

Till all is said and done, our earth (particularly the Middle East in the next few years) might look like "Jericho Revisited

Part 2." Stay tuned. Before God is through, He will make Cecil B. DeMille's great epic *The Ten Commandments* look like cartoons. He will complete His righteous judgments and restoration for all the nations. Drama and action take place when God gets involved. It's all in His Book. A generation will be swept into God's love and safety in less time than it takes to build a house. Watch for it. This is the hour of God's visitation. Better put on "His robe of righteousness" if you want to be dressed and ready when company arrives. Forget the big department stores, all you need is to purchase from Him "fine garments and white linens." Pray and seek the Living God and His Son Jesus. That's all it takes. Turn off the world and spend those hours talking to Him. You'll know God, and when you have Him, you have everything.

"I am pregnant with the season of the Lord, and I will give birth to a summer child." Selah.

Warning to America

In late August of 1983 I woke up in the middle of the night to find the room lit with the power of God. As John the Revelator said, "Whether in the spirit or in the flesh, I do not know." I only know that I saw Jesus Christ break through the eastern sky as the prophet saw Him riding through the sky with tens of thousands of saints riding behind Him. As one would watch a 3-D event, it was as if my eyes could see in the distance—and the face of Christ approached me as if He burst into the room.

I now know what the gospel writer meant when He said, "I fell at His feet as though I were dead." I remember being so overtaken with a sense of His holiness, I felt totally naked. Undone. It is the only way to describe the face I saw. He did not look like the gentle little lamb we see on Christmas cards with the cherub face, but rather a burning gaze that will unravel the soul not covered with the Passover blood, the blood of Messiah—Jesus Christ. His hair was white as snow and His eyes burned like fire; He said, not with words, but spoke in His eyes—and I KNEW what He meant. He said, "Tell them I am coming."

The next thing I remember was that I was sitting up in bed and felt as if I sat between two worlds. It was the strangest feeling I had ever had. I had this deep sense of peace flooding through me, yet an urgency not only to repent, but to tell others to also. A while later, the phone rang. The Lord had told a Christian friend that He was going to speak to me. In fact, she was not as surprised as I thought she would be at what I told her. The next few weeks were uncanny confirmations by co-workers, friends, and others that something very unusual had happened.

* * * * * *

In 1985, I would experience another revealing dream that I still remember. It was during the fall, when the nights were cool, and I went to sleep like any other night. This night when I awoke, I didn't know if I was dreaming or listening to the radio alarm clock on the night table along side of my bed turn on. I heard the announcer clearly yet nervously say, "This is not a test, this is a national emergency. Russian bombers have just passed over New York City and are heading across the East!"

I remember sitting up in bed, and I could hear (in my spirit) the sounds of jets going overhead. I then looked at the clock; it was early, before the sun rose in most Eastern states. I remember thinking, *Did this just happen, or am I dreaming?* I sat in bed motionless for a few minutes. My senses could hardly take in all I was feeling at that moment.

As I got out of bed, I realized this was not my imagination but my spirit seeing something very real. I did not know when this would happen, but I knew it was not only in my lifetime, but in America's imminent future.

I relayed this event to several Christian friends who seemed to understand how very real this event was to me. Scripture references are Maccabees 2:7 (NEB version)[1],

---

1.   **New English Bible**, © Oxford University Press and Cambridge University Press 1961, 1970.

Psalm 68:4, Daniel 7:13, Matthew 24:30, Revelation 1:7. In the next seven to ten years, this "night vision" was confirmed in many ways through the testimony of God's people.

The Scripture references that I believe apply to this dream are from the book of Jeremiah chapter 50, verses 9, 23, and 40. In chapter 14 of Jeremiah, verses 12 and 13, there stands the prophet talking of sword (war), famine and pestilence that overtook the nation (Israel) that God had loved so much yet that had forsaken His covenant. This democracy we live in has much similarity to the theocracy that first bore the covenant: Israel and America's destinies are tied through the blood lines of Abraham through all the promises made to his seed.

God showed me that America, like Israel, was established by promises to God, oaths and covenants. Israel was a government of theocracy and was to be governed by God. The best example of this government was in the life of David—priest, prophet and king. The Republic, America, was established with a democracy and set of laws so wise that only God was given the honor for the institution of these laws. Our nations' founding documents bear this in parchment.

The Lord circles the land and the people He loves like a fire. Who can touch them, if THEY are right with the Lord?

I believe it was during the fall of the next year that I had another dream that was so real, it too woke me up. In the dream, my bed which was against the eastern wall of the house was pushed down by a gush of water which can only be compared to a tidal wave. I had no fear in this dream. I knew I was being miraculously protected. The gushing deluge of water overtook everything in sight, but the bed I was on was raised high up, above the water, to rest on the crest of the wave that the water made. I knew I was safe. There was a baby in a little bed along side of me, and I didn't know what the baby represented. The following is the interpretation the Lord gave me on the dream:

The tidal wave is the outpouring gush of revival that will soon hit the earth—the revival is now in the earth—but the power of the Spirit of God which propels the gospel to be preached is going to be magnified. The church of Jesus Christ in the earth today will ride the crest of the wave of the next move of God's spirit. The baby on the bed was the Christ child: the birth of God's power, the gospel being preached, the revival of the church, that man-child (Pentecost Power of the church) going forth.

September, 1990. It was during the second week when I awoke at 3:00 a.m. and was aware that the presence of God had filled the room. I lay motionless on my bed—unable to even open my mouth to pray. It was as if the hand of the Lord came down on me, and I had the most incredible burden for America! God gave me a Scripture from the Old Testament, and I knew that was for America. The Lord also pressed on my spirit with such intensity; I wondered why. I had a sense of a soul falling into hell's fire, and it was so painful I could not stand it. It was as if the pain took my breath away. I think it only lasted a few seconds—but it was anguish.

The Lord gave me the Scripture Jeremiah chapter 25 for America. I knew God was serious, and He would deal severely with America in the days ahead. One only has to look at the news and realize God is already dealing seriously with America. Looking at Jeremiah 9:7 and 9:10, we see that the fire God is speaking of is a very real burning of the flesh. A very real desolation. It makes the movie "The Day After" very real in its portrayal of judgment. Oh, it may look like nations against nations, but God uses evil nations as His weapons. He says it over and over in His Word. Read Jeremiah 4:19 and Jeremiah 8:20, and you will understand what the burden for one living soul means to God.

In the Scripture Jeremiah 25:29, God says, "I will call for a sword upon all the inhabitants of the earth." Whether the prophet foretold of World War III or not, I don't know. I only know God's fury will be unleashed in the coming days. I know His mercy. His powerful love, and His deepest desire is that not one perish, but that all repent and come to His salvation. Before the major earthquake that will rock the earth (Is. 24:19-20), there will be many "spiritual" earthquakes that will shake off the sleep from the Church and cause God's people to wake up and get their lamps trimmed with oil (see Mt.25:1)—the oil of the Holy Spirit. Jeremiah 6:11 is a strong warning to the U.S.A. I believe the latter part of the tribulation period is when Jeremiah chapter 50 is to be fulfilled. The judgment to fall on all nations is recorded in Isaiah 14:26. When the day of the Lord comes (Zechariah chapter 14), Christ will come in all of His Kingship, to dismantle corrupt governments, Himself fighting against that which would war against His Kingdom. There will be a division against the spiritually blind, against those who know His Lordship, against those who trust world systems and those who trust God's Son. All who call upon the name of the Lord shall be saved.

Is there hope? Absolutely. Until the flood came, there was hope for all who were alive during Noah's day. For almost 100 years Noah preached while many scorned his words. He and his family were saved because they entered the ark of the covenant before the flood came. TODAY, all alive can enter the ARK OF THE COVENANT, Jesus Christ, through faith and trust in Jesus Christ. For all flesh alive today, the word is in Amos 4:12—REPENT and be saved. Especially the church—go "back to your first love."

"He will shout like those who tread the grapes, shout against all who live on the earth." (Jer. 25:30c NIV.) Are these the grapes of wrath that will turn the world into a winepress of affliction? "A tumult will resound to the ends of the earth, for the Lord will bring charges against the nations." (Jer. 25:31 NIV.) Is this the sound of nuclear war that will usher in the end of man's war against God and herald the beginning of a new reign, the millennial reign of Christ?

I can tell you, I understand why Jeremiah is often referred to as "the weeping prophet" by some Bible scholars. You would cry, too, if God chose to press in on your soul for the souls of others. How would you react if you lived through what Hosea, Jeremiah, or other saints lived through? What about the sufferings of John and his subsequent banishment to the isle of Patmos? You might think, "What a dream, to see the future," but I think, "What a price he paid to even get there." The price, dear friend, is your flesh. Your soul. Christ becomes everything, layer by layer, peeling by peeling, trial by fire. What would you do if the Lord appeared to you? What would you do if your faith put you on the witness stand, meant having a few pebbles thrown at you, or resulted in a long suffering for a people you could not explain away? What did the early Church do? They trusted in His name—we have His name and His grace. No one survives faith's trials without grace.

See if your 'life plans' change, destiny is reshaped, hopes are deferred, burdens increase and substance of all that you see is seen differently, as when seen through the eyes of faith.

A good word to the Church of Jesus Christ in this hour is: there is a redemption ahead, and yes, there is a resurrection. God loves and longs to pour out His glory and healing power and ever-present hope through His Church. But know this, the cross came before the resurrection. If you think anyone will or can carry the cross for you, you're deceiving yourself. The wisdom of a 70-year-old cannot be transplanted into a seven-year-old by osmosis; the beauty and wisdom that the Church will reveal in the very imminent future before the return of her King will require and demand startling choices, life-changing encounters, and unshakable faith. How will the Church survive without His grace? It cannot do anything apart from Him.

And for Israel (spiritual and natural) God's love is as strong as ever. He will find no more guilt in her, as He says in Jeremiah 50:20. He will guard her, and protect her, and cause her name to last forever. God is married to Israel, and His feet will rush to protect her. The Messiah's feet will touch the Temple in Zion, and He will be her God.

The Lord birthed this song for all who believe in the God of the covenant.

Remnant of Jehovah

"We are a remnant for Jehovah,
we are a remnant for our God.
The Lord Christ dwells within,
we are a remnant for our God.

I am a daughter of Abraham,
I am the sister of St. Paul.
By faith am I in covenant
with the Lord who made us all.

I am a remnant for Jehovah,
I am a remnant for my God."

E. Mary Mickel
© 1983

They're Just Doing Their Job

The gospel states that the angels in heaven rejoice when a sinner repents and inherits eternal life. The angels even long to understand the mysteries of our salvation (1 Peter 1:12 NIV).

God's protective covering enables us to receive the protection of these heavenly *bodyguards*, yet we are not to worship or focus on them, as both men and angels were created by God to worship Him alone (Hebrews 1:14, Psalm 91:11, Colossians 2:18 NIV).

There is a lot of focus on the angelic realm today, yet they are only doing their job: worshipping God in obedience.

The Samaritan Anointing

I have a wonderful dinner companion who phones me from time to time; our friendship spans almost a score of years. We've shared home-baked bread from the corner bakery, but the best meal we share is the "hidden manna" that the Lord Jesus promised to give those who love Him (Rev. 2:17). This meal is already paid for (Calvary's expense account). It is the food of God: His life is in it.

My old friend discovered long ago that playing church is not real religion, nor is a zillion good works redemptive (unless God's Spirit is in it). Walking in the Spirit and denying the flesh isn't about being morbid and doing mitzvahs till you drop, or about impossible religious laws that only end in weariness (the flesh is death because His joy and life are not in it). Walking in the Spirit is about the fragrance and joy of the Holy Spirit working through you and in you—to allow His life to flow (where real joy and peace come from).

You can spend hours in churches that weigh you down with laws, you can tithe your heart out, do Girl Scouts on Monday, choir on Tuesday, drive kids to Little League on Wednesday, visit the nursing home on Thursday, and be drop-dead tired and wonder why there is no joy in it all. Or, you can be free from the expectations of others, yourself and the weariness of busyness, and just do as the Lord did—be led by the Spirit—to go where and pick up the load He does. Nothing more. The life of Jesus was amazingly free of clutter and vain attempts to try and add to anything that God was not really in.

Jesus said "I do nothing on my own but speak just what the Father has taught me" (John 8:28 NIV).

It isn't that there are not good and necessary services to do in serving God as a believer; it is that unless we leave the "Martha" mentality that Jesus spoke of and put on the fresh life of "Mary," we'll miss the freedom of this walk God wanted to give us (Lk. 10:38-42). Serving God with joy, power, and peace is only possible when we are drinking from His well. You can go 18 hours a day—if God gives you the strength for the occasion, if you love what you're doing; He'll give you the strength. Conversely, if you're doing good works and keeping busy, but your heart isn't in it, you'll tire more easily without His (the Lord's) grace.

For me, a lesson God is still teaching me is to learn what it is He wants of me. God is a better manager of time and resources, and a far better planner than we are. There are times you can do far more for God and yourself by just taking the phone off the hook, going for a walk, or taking the wife and kids for an ice cream cone and a hike. And there are times that you'll have to pray in tears and spend time in His Word, or take that evening to go to that service and worship Him with the saints. The point is: Christianity is not about how much you do for God (quantity), it is about quality. The greatest in the Kingdom are often the least (Jesus' words). The Marys are focusing on her Lord's needs and heart. Find out yourself what God made you for; find out from God (not your pastor or friend or anyone else) what He wants from your life and relationships. He'll show you. He'll guide you and speak to your heart, and there is such freedom in that.

For years, I had a problem knowing it was okay to say "no." Believers in Christ need to learn that Jesus said "no" to the enemy of His flesh (in the wilderness), to the expectation of society (they wanted a king to get the show off the road), and that many times, after an anointed service, He simply picked up His gear and left. He learned to say "no" when family, religious leaders and even His dearest friends tried to steer Him off course, the course He knew He had to follow. Saying "no" in love is not rebellion; it is true liberty. Wherever we are not free to truly express the life of God in us as God made us, we are in bondage to the flesh.

Jesus was never in bondage to the flesh because He had no fear of man. No one's opinion mattered more to Him than His Father's, and since He had no sin in Him, the perfect love in Him left no room for the devil to plant thoughts of insecurity, pride, doubt, or anxiety. The Bible tells us that the blessings of God are Yea and Amen in Christ Jesus. We can be certain that it is our Father's desire to bring to each one of us the wholeness and identity that is ours in Christ Jesus. By His own blood, Christ purchased for His Church her complete identity in Him. *When you know who you are, there is no fear to hold you to what you are not.*

A dear friend and I have enjoyed the kind of friendship that can only be from God. When God "knits" hearts in one accord, there is no room for division. We are free to agree as well as disagree. No two friends, mates, co-workers or parent and child will be exactly alike (thank God for the freedom of uniqueness). Even in an old friendship—when you are able to accept another without false expectations and your commitment to another's well-being is not tantamount to performance—you can grow to a place of trust, of becoming whole with another person. This is really what heaven is like: intimacy without the sin strains of our human personality. It is what every soul longs for: the intimacy God intended. When you love someone (whether you're understood or not) you have come to a place of rest (see Ex. 33:14, Ps. 62:1, Heb. 4:10) where you and another are free from expectation and need for approval.

Imagine going to your job and enjoying it. Ever notice when you're doing something you really love, it comes easy. The anointing or grace is there, and it flows. Be it skiing, cooking, jogging, laughing, telling a good joke, rocking a baby, working in the garden, whatever, there is a rest when we are able to flow in the gift God gave us. The greatest inventions, moments of genius, ideas (like, "Where did that come from?)," and feelings of joy come when you don't plan it (flesh), but when you are walking out your identity in Him (like Jesus lived) and the Father in Heaven pours out His spectacular glory into your every day.

Truly, when sin entered the world, we lost our rest. We toil (Adam's curse) with insecurity and striving, and birth our works (like Eve) in labor because pain has entered where once the birthing of joy and glory was easy. Now can you see what Jesus' blood really bought back for us? Our covering. The joy of our work, the joy of relationships, the blessings of intimacy, the fulfillment and completeness that was meant to be in every area of our lives, all this, Christ is restoring as it was meant to be.

This, dear soul, is the hidden manna. When you can come up to a complete stranger, not say another word but "Hi," and feel the power of God's love touch someone, you can see it in their eyes—they know it is something good—they just don't know it's God. This is the parable of the Good Samaritan. Sometimes strangers and those who don't know God have blessed me with kindness that I knew came from God. They were being used of God, whether they knew Him or not.

Since there is no righteousness in the flesh, walking in the Spirit means putting on the mind of Christ (Rom. 12:2) and walking away from our old ways of death. The term "flesh" doesn't mean our skin, but the heart and mind attitudes, our reasoning and ways that are different from God's. Walking in the Spirit doesn't make you a statue or a goody-two-shoes, it makes you real and makes your feet stand solid wherever your shoes take you. Walking in the Spirit makes you whole.

* My prayer for all who read this is that we all may come to know the rest that Jesus Christ the Lord promises to those who desire to walk with Him: the rest that always refreshes (Rev. 14:13).

No human institution can *truly* qualify you for sainthood, it is the blood of Jesus Christ which has sanctified the lives of all those who believe (Mt. 26:28, Ro. 3:25, Eph. 1:7, Hebrews 9:12, John 6:53, 1 Pe. 1:19, Rev. 1:5 NIV).

Who can purchase His Kingdom, but the King?

Chapter 2

It All Started
in a Garden

They have asked us to refrain from teaching our children about God. "Just look how those Christians try and 'sneak' the creation theory into the schools. Creationism (it sounds too definite, I presume, just to be called 'creation') is to the learned, a theory passed down through the generations, like all traditions, by some doting old grandmother-types who were either too unafraid or too unschooled to venture out into the real world of modern thinkers and challenge the absoluteness of this 'myth.' "

I suppose, then, I must address myself to the "learned," for it is certainly inconceivable to me that 100 trillion cells in the human body (each capable of maintaining life on its own and reproducing itself) just appeared at some random point in time.

Is it also within reason to believe that 206 bones, miles and miles of an intricate muscular-skeletal organization, an interdependent network of valves, vessels, veins and organs, and much more, just happened by chance to connect itself together perfectly, and to work, with more accuracy and effectiveness, than a finely tuned machine?

I suppose the millions of beats our heart gives during a lifetime, all part of an incredible involuntary response of a perfected muscle, and the ability of the immune system's power for self-healing is just a happening of chance through years of animal evolution?

The only myth I expose is that rational, thinking men could assume that all this matter just evolved and happened to work in harmony by chance or time, rather than to give an omnipotent sovereignty the credit for it. To me, the blindest act for a thinking man is to deny Genesis.

Photosynthesis, reproduction, the miracle of light and its effect on all living things, and even the laws of nature should be evidence enough for a man of reason to accept a divine intervention into the scheme of living things. But then, I conclude Martin Luther was right when he said, "Reason is the greatest enemy faith has; it never comes to the aid of spiritual things, but more frequently than not, struggles against the divine Word, treating with contempt all that emanates from God." I often believed a child knew far more about God than the working and thoughts of all academia, for the necessary key to unlocking knowledge of God is through faith. After all, doesn't the first law of thermodynamics state "Energy can be changed from one form to another, but it cannot be created or destroyed."[1] I suppose man would even conceptualize Genesis if he could. Divinity is a state of being that the author of life began Himself. If your modern mind cannot accept this, you are not enlightened. You are denying your own identity. To deny Genesis is the first deceit against you. "By dividing body and soul, we divide both from all else. We thus condemn ourselves to a loneliness for which the only compensation is violence—against other creatures, against the earth, against ourselves. For no matter the distinctions we

---

1. Helena Curtis, *Invitation to Biology*. (New York, N.Y.: Worth Publishers, 1972), p. 85.

draw between body and soul, body and earth, ourselves and others—the connections, the dependencies, the identities remain."[2]

The cycles of man can be measured with an almost arithmetic certainty, yet the destinies of the generations of men belong to the spirit of God.

As every generation repeats the pattern of weakness to strength, life to death, and for the believe—glory to glory, the Creator of all things is always at work to restore all things to His original dream: the garden (Gen. 2:8, John 5:17, Gen. 2:15, Ezekiel 28:13, Eze. 31:9).

---

2.   Wendell Berry, *The Unsettling of America: Culture and Agriculture* (New York: Avon Books, 1979), p. 106.

"Let us go then, you and I,
When the evening is spread out against the sky
Like a patient etherized upon a table."[3]

Taken from:
The Love Song of J. Alfred Prufrock
T.S. Eliot

---

3.   T.S. Eliot, The Love Song of J. Alfred Prufrock. *The Norton Anthology of American Literature* (New York, New York: W.W. Norton & Co., 1979), p. 1219.

"He made me unhappy. But He has also allowed me to know a happiness passing all understanding. He has, and I must not forget it.

What would my life be without him? If I had never been filled with Him, with his Spirit? If I had never felt the bliss that poured from Him, the anguish and pain that is His also, and the wonder of being annihilated in His blazing arms, of being altogether His? Of feeling His rapture, His boundless bliss, and sharing God's infinite happiness in being alive?

What would I have been without that? If I had never experienced anything but myself?"[4]

Taken from:
The Sibyl
Pär Lagerkvist

---

4. Par Lagerkvist, *The Sibyl.* (New York, N.Y.: Vintage Books, Radom House, 1958), p. 150.

The Raven Days

"Our hearts are gone out, and our hearts are broken,
And but the ghosts of homes to us remain,
And ghostly eyes and hollow sighs give token
From friend to friend of an unspoken pain.

O, Raven Days, dark Raven Days of sorrow,
Bring to us, in your whetted ivory beaks,
Some sign out of the far land of To-morrow,
Some strip of sea-green dawn, some orange streaks.

Ye float in dusky files, forever croaking—
Ye chill our manhood with your dreary shade.
Pale, in the dark, not even God invoking,
We lie in chains, too weak to be afraid.

O Raven Days, dark Raven Days of sorrow,
Will ever any warm light come again?
Will ever the lit mountains of To-morrow
Begin to gleam across the mournful plain?[5]

The Raven Days
Sidney Lanier

---

5.   Sidney Lanier, The Raven Days, *The Oxford Book of American Verse.* (New York, N.Y.: Oxford University Press, 1950), p. 444.

"O Lily of the King! I speak of heavy thing,
O patience, most sorrowful of daughters!
Lo, the hour is at hand for the troubling of the land,
And the red shall be the breaking of the waters.

Sit fast upon thy stalk, when the blast with thee shall talk,
With the just understand thine hour is at hand,
Thine hour at hand with power in the dawning.
When the nations lie in blood, and their kings a broken brood,
Look up, O most sorrowful of daughters!
Lift up thy head and hark what sound are in the dark,
For his feet are coming to thee on the waters."[6]

Lilium Regis
Francis Thompson

---

6.   Francis Thompson, *The Hound of Heaven and other poems by Francis Thompson*. (Boston: International Pocket Library, 1936), pp. 29,30.

On that day there will be no light, no cold or frost. It will be a unique day, without daytime or nighttime—a day known to the Lord. When evening comes, there will be light. The Lord will be King over the whole earth. On that day there will be one Lord, and His name the only name.

Zechariah 14:6-7,9 NIV[7]

---

7. Scripture quotations marked (NIV) are taken from the **Holy Bible, New International Version** ® NIV® Copyright © 1973, 1978, 1984 by International Bible Society. Used by permission of Zondervan Publishing House. All rights reserved.

You are the light of the world. A city on a hill cannot be hidden.

Matthew 5:14 NIV

"Go into all the world and preach the good news to all creation. Whoever believes and is baptized will be saved, but whoever does not believe will be condemned."

Mark 16:15-16 NIV

"Man, introverted man, having crossed in passage
   and but a little with the nature of things
   this latter century
Has begot giants; but being taken up
Like a maniac with self-love and inward conflicts
   cannot manage his hybrids.
Being used to deal with edgeless dreams,
Now he's bred knives on nature turns them
   also inward: they have thirsty points though.
His mind forebodes his own destruction;
Actaeon who saw the goddess naked among
   leaves and his hounds tore him.
A little knowledge, a pebble from the shingle,
A drop from the oceans: who would have
   dreamed this infinitely little too much?"[8]

"Science"
Robinson Jeffers

---

8.   Jeffers, Science, Science, *Oxford Books*, p. 783. From The Selected Poetry of Robinson Jeffers by Robinson Jeffers © 1925 and
renewed 1953 by Robinson Jeffers. Reprinted by permission of
Random House, Inc.

You will hear of wars and rumors of wars. Do not be alarmed. Such things are bound to happen, but that is not yet the end.

Matthew 24:6 NIV

But the day of the Lord will come as a thief in the night; in the which the heavens shall pass away with a great noise, and the elements shall melt with fervent heat, the earth also and the works that are therein shall be burned up.

2 Peter 3:10 NIV

Now faith is being sure of what we hope for and certain of what we do not see. This is what the ancients were commended for. All these people were still living by faith when they died. They did not receive the things promised, they only saw them and welcomed them from a distance.

Hebrews 11:1-2,13 NIV

Then I saw the beast, and the kings of the earth, and their armies, gathered together to make war against Him that sat on the horse, and against His army. And the beast was taken and with him the false prophet that wrought miracles performed in before him, with which he deceived them that had received the mark of the beast, and them that worshipped his image. These both were cast down alive into a lake of fire burning with brimstone. And the remnant were slain with the sword of Him that sat upon the horse, which sword proceeded out of his mouth: and all the fowls were filled with their flesh.

Revelation 19:19-21 NIV

"In a dark time, the eye begins to see,
I meet my shadow in the deepening shade;
I hear my echo in the echoing wood—
A lord of nature weeping to a tree.
I live between the heron the wren,
Beasts of the hill and serpents of the den.

What's madness but nobility of the soul
At odds with circumstance? The day's on fire!
I know the purity of pure despair,
My shadow pinned against a sweating wall.
That place among the rocks—is it a cave,
Or winding path? The edge is what I have.

A steady storm of correspondence!
A night flowing with birds, a ragged moon,
And in broad day the midnight comes again!
A man goes far to find out what he is—
Death of the self in a long, tearless night,
All natural shapes blazing unnatural light.

Dark, dark my light, and darker my desire.
My soul, like some heat-maddened summer fly,
Keeps buzzing at the sill. Which I is I?
A fallen man, I climb out of my fear.
The mind enters itself, and God the mind,
And one is One, free in the tearing wind."[9]

"In a Dark Time"
Theodore Roethke

---

9.   Theodore Roethke et al., eds., *In a Dark Time, The Norton Anthology of American Literature.* (New York: W.W. Norton and Company, 1979), p. 2,267.

51

Then I saw the heavens and a new earth. The former heavens and the former earth had passed away, and the sea was no longer. I also saw a new Jerusalem, the holy city, coming down out of heaven from God, beautiful as a bride prepared to meet her husband. I heard a loud voice from the throne cry out: "This is God's dwelling among men. He shall dwell with them and they shall be his people and he shall be their God who is always with them. He shall wipe every tear from their eyes, and there shall be no more death or mourning, crying out or pain, for the former world has passed away."

Revelation 21:1-4 NIV

"Deep in the greens of summer sings the lives
I've come to love. A vireo whets its bill.
The great day balances upon the leaves;
My ears still hear the bird when all is still;
My soul is still my soul, and still the Son,
And knowing this, I am yet undone.

Things without hands take hands: there is no choice—
Eternity's not easily come by.
When opposites come suddenly in place,
I teach my eyes to hear, my ears to see
How body from spirit slowly does unwind
Until we are pure spirit at the end."[10]

Taken from:
"Infirmity"
Theodore Roethke

---

10. Roethke et al., eds., Infirmity, *The Norton Anthology of American Literature.* (New York: W.W. Norton and Company, 1979), p. 2,273.

Tell Them I Am Coming

"And God said / Prophesy to the wind, to the wind
only for only / the wind will listen."[11]

Taken from:
"Ash-Wednesday"
by T.S. Eliot

---

11. T.S. Eliot, Ash-Wednesday, *Oxford Book of Verse*, p. 820. Taken
from: Ash-Wednesday by T.S. Eliot, *From Collected Poems by
T.S. Eliot* (1909-1962). © 1930. Used by permission of Harcourt
Brace & Co. Publishers, U.S.A.

A message to Zion: *"Hear O Israel, The Lord Our God Is One"* (Shamoi Israel, Adonai El O Henu Adonai ER HAD)

"The quality of mercy is not strain'd, it droppeth
as the gentle rain from heaven
Upon the place beneath: it is twice bless'd;
It blesseth him that gives and him that takes:
'Tis mightiest in the mightiest; it becomes
The Throned monarch better than his crown;
His scepter shows the force of temporal power,
The attribute to awe and majesty,
Wherein doth sit the dread and fear of kings;
But mercy is above the scepter'd sway,
It is enthroned in the hearts of kings,
It is an attribute to God himself,
An earthly power doth then show liketh God's
When mercy seasons justice. Therefore, Jew,
Though justice by thy plea, consider this,
That in the course of justice, none of us
Should see salvation: we do pray for mercy,
And that same prayer doth teach us all to
render the deeds of mercy."[12]

Taken from:
"The Merchant of Venice"
William Shakespeare

---

12. William Aldis Wright, *The Complete Works of William Shakespeare*, Cambridge ed. text. (Garden City, N.Y: Garden City Publishing Company, 1936), p. 469.

The Road Not Taken

I shall be telling this with a sigh
Somewhere ages and ages hence:
Two roads diverged in a wood, and I—
I took the one less traveled by,
And that has made the difference.[13]

Taken from:
"The Road Not Taken"
Robert Frost

---

13. Frost, The Road Not Taken, The Norton Anthology, pp. 1117-1118. Taken From The Road Not Taken, *The Poetry of Robert Frost*, ed. by Edward Connery Lathem, © 1916, 1967, 1969 by Holt, Rinehart Winston, Henry Holt & Co., Inc., N.Y., N.Y.

Faith

"It was mercy that nailed Jesus to the cross. God's mercy for us, poured out in love, through Christ."

Author unknown

I solemnly assure you, said Jesus, "The man who hears My word and has faith in Him who sent Me possesses eternal life."

John 5:24 NAB

The man who believes in it and accepts baptism will be saved; the man who refuses to believe in it will be condemned.

Mark 16:16 NAB

Yes, God so loved the world that He gave His only Son, that whomever believes in Him may not die, but have eternal life.

John 3:16 NAB

I repeat, it is owing to His favor that salvation is yours through faith. This is not your own doing, it is God's gift.

Ephesians 2:8 NAB

Sanctified Life

Not everyone who says to Me, "Lord, Lord," will enter into the Kingdom of Heaven, but only he who does the will of My Father in Heaven.

Matthew 7:21 NIV

The Son of Man will come with His Father's glory accompanied by His angels. When He does, He will repay each man according to his conduct.

Matthew 16:27 NIV

Do you now know that God's kindness is an invitation to you to repent? In spite of this, your hard and impenitent heart is storing up retribution for that day of wrath when the just judgment of God will be revealed, when He will repay every man for what he has done: eternal life for those who strive for glory, honor, and immortality by patiently doing right; wrath for those who selfishly disobey the truth and obey wickedness.

Romans 2:4-8 NAB

In mythology, a generation was cursed with unbelief because of Cassandra. In reality, God tells us He will close their ears to hear and their eyes to see, if they continue to rebel and not listen.

And if anyone tells you, "This is the Messiah," or "That one is," don't pay any attention. For there will be many false messiahs and false prophets who would do wonderful miracles that would deceive, even if possible, God's own children. Take care. I have warned you.

Mark 13:21 NAB

At that time the sign of the Son of Man will appear in the sky, and all the nations of the earth will mourn. They will see the Son of Man coming on the clouds of the sky, with power and great glory.

Mt. 24:30 NIV

Watch

Matthew 24:40-51; Mark 13; Luke 21; Matthew 22:1-14, 25:1-13; Luke 14:16-24; Matthew 13:24-30, 22:13, 24:51, 25:30, 3:12, 13:30; Luke 3:17; Mark 9:48; Matthew 18:9; Mark 9:46-47; Matthew 18:7-9; Luke 16:19-31; Matthew 7:13-14, 24:40-41, 25:30; Luke 16:28; Romans 2:8 NIV

His Return

Daniel 7:13; Matthew 25:31-46; Mark 13:26-27; Acts 1:11; 1 Corinthians 15:22-23; I Thessalonians 4:6-17; 2 Timothy 4:8; James 5:7-9; I Thessalonians 5:2; 2 Peter 3:10. The Lord has given us His bread for life.

"For as the lightning comes from the east and shines as far as the west, so will be the coming of the Son of Man" (Mt. 24:27 NIV).

Do not be like Faustus who did not listen to the good angel on his left saying, "Turn to God."

Listen, and Live.

Chapter 3

The Surrender

The First Day's Night Had Come

"The first Day's Night had come—
And, grateful that a thing
So terrible had been endured,
I told my Soul to sing.

She said her strings were snapt,
her bow to atoms blown;
And so, to mend her, gave me work
Until another morn.

And then a Day as huge
As Yesterday in pairs
Unrolled its horror on my face—
Until it blocked my eyes."[1]

Emily Dickinson

---

1.   Emily Dickinson, The First Day's Night Had Come, *Oxford Book*, p. 422. From **The Complete Poems of Emily Dickinson** edited by Thomas H. Johnson. © 1929, 1935 by Martha Dickinson Bianchi; renewed 1957, 1963 by Mary L. Hampson. By permission Little, Brown & Company.

A fire devoureth before them, and behind them a flame burneth into desolate wilderness; yea, and nothing shall escape.

Joel 2:3 KJV

Ample Make This Bed

"Ample make this bed.
Make this bed with awe;
In it wait till judgment break
Excellent and fair.

Be its mattress straight,
Be its pillow round;
Let no sunrise yellow noise
Interrupt this ground."[2]

Emily Dickinson

---

2. Dickinson, Ample Make This Bed, *Oxford Book*, p. 440. From **The Complete Poems of Emily Dickinson.**

For all creation is waiting patiently and hopefully for that future day when God will resurrect His children. For on that day thorns and thistles, sin and death, and decay, the things that overcame the world against its will at God's command will all disappear, and the world around us will share in the glorious freedom from sin which God's children will enjoy. For we know that all creation groaneth, the things of nature, like animals and plants, suffer in sickness and death (but these are labor pains) as they wait this great Event.

Romans 8:19-22
New Jerusalem Bible

Because I Could Not Stop For Death

"Because I could not stop for Death,
He kindly stopped for me;
The carriage held but just ourselves
And Immortality.

We slowly drove, he knew no haste,
And I had put away
My labor, and my leisure too,
For his civility.

We passed the school where children played
At wrestling in a ring;
We passed the fields of gazing grain,
We passed the setting sun.

We paused before a house that seemed
A swelling of the ground;
The roof was scarcely visible,
The cornice but a mound.

Since then 'tis centuries; but each
Feels shorter than the day
I first surmised the horses' heads
Were toward eternity."[3]

Emily Dickinson

---

3.   Dickinson, Because I Could Not Stop For Death, *Oxford Book*,
      p. 439. From **The Complete Poems of Emily Dickinson** and Re-
      printed by permission of the publishers and the Trustees of Am-
      herst College From **The Poems of Emily Dickinson**, Thomas H.
      Johnson, ed., Cambridge, MASS.: The Belknap Press of Harvard
      University Press, © 1951, 1955, 1979, 1983 by the Residents and
      Fellows of Harvard College.

Being born again, not of corruptible seed, but of in-corruptible, by the Word of God, which liveth and abideth forever. For all flesh is as grass, and all the glory of man as the flower of grass. The grass withereth, and the flower thereof falleth away: but the word of the Lord endureth forever...

1 Peter 1:23-25 KJV

The End of the World

"Quite unexpectedly as Vasserot
The armless ambidextrian was lighting
A match between his great and second toe
And Ralph the lion was engaged in biting
The neck of Madame Sossman while the drum
Pointed, and Teeny was about to cough
In waltz-time swinging Jocko by the thumb—
Quite unexpectedly the top blew off:

And there, there overhead, there, there, hung over
Those thousands of white faces, those dazed eyes,
there in the starless dark the poise, the hover,
There with vast wings across the cancelled skies,
There in the sudden blackness the black pall
Of nothing, nothing, nothing—nothing at all."[4]

Taken from:
The End of the World
Archibald MacLeish

---

4.   MacLeish, The End of the World, *Oxford Book*, p. 892.

And except those days be shortened, there should no flesh be saved: but for the elect's sake those days shall be shortened.

Matthew 24:22 KJV

Daybreak

To find the Western path,
Right through the Gates of Wrath
I urge my way;
Sweet Mercy leads me on
With soft repentant moan:
I see the break of day.[5]

Taken from:
Daybreak
William Blake

5.   Wallace A. Briggs, *Great Poems of the English Language*. (New York, N.Y: Tudor Publishing Co., 1936), p. 336.

For there shall arise false Christs, and false prophets, and shall shew great signs and wonders; insomuch that, if it were possible, they shall deceive the very elect. Behold, I have told you before. Wherefore if they shall say unto you, Behold, he is in the desert; go not forth: behold, he is in the secret chambers; believe it not. For as the lightning cometh out of the east, and shineth even unto the west; so shall also the coming of the Son of man be.

Matthew 24:24-27 KJV

Address to My Soul

"My soul, be not disturbed
by planetary war;
Remain securely orbed
In this contracted star.

Fear not, pathetic flame;
Your sustenance is doubt,
Glassed in translucent dream
They cannot snuff you out."[6]

Taken from:
Address to My Soul
Elinor Wylie

---

6. From **Collected Poems** by Elinor Wylie © 1928 by Alfred A.
    Knopf Inc. and renewed 1956 by Edwina C. Rubenstein. Reprinted
    by permission of the publisher.

The Grapes of Wrath

"And they stand still and watch the potatoes float by, listen to the screaming pigs being killed in a ditch and covered with quicklime, watch the mountains of oranges slope down to a putrefying ooze; and in the eyes of the people there is the failure; and in the eyes of the hungry there is a growing wrath. In the souls of the people the grapes of wrath are filling and growing heavy, growing heavy for the vintage."[7]

Taken from:
The Grapes of Wrath
John Steinbeck

---

7. From **The Grapes of Wrath** by John Steinbeck. Copyright 1939, renewed © 1967 by John Steinbeck. Used by permission of Viking Penguin Books USA Inc.

"All those monsters come into the world only to stimulate the courage of the children of God, and when they have finished their training, God allows them to slay the monster. Heaven receives the victors and hell engulfs the vanquished. A new monster appears and God summons fresh monsters into the arena. Our life here is a spectacle which makes heaven rejoice, rears up saints and confounds hell. And so all that opposes the rule of God only succeeds it more worthy of being adored. All the enemies of justice become its slaves, and God builds the heavenly Jerusalem with the fragments of Babylon destroyed."[8]

Taken from:
Abandonment to Divine Providence
Jean-Pierra de Caussade

8. Jean-Pierra de Caussade, *Abandonment to Divine Providence.* (New York: N.Y: Doubleday Publ. 1966), p. 119.

XXXI

"The patient is killed by a bomb and slips through Worm-wood's fingers. Though the letter is ostensibly about Screw-tape's picture of the horrors awaiting Wormwood, it is really an unintentional tribute to God's triumphant love, and so rich in praise that it beggars even those works which set out to do precisely this. The Beatific Vision which Screwtape and other devils forfeited because of their pride they must now observe being enjoyed by what was once a 'mere' mortal. 'This animal, this thing begotten in a bed,' as Screwtape calls the patient, has exchanged his body of clay for a glorious body no less immortal than that of the Risen Saviour. As he passes into the happy land of the Trinity, notice that the pa-tient says, not 'Who are you?' but 'so it was *you* all the time.' And after that? As Lewis has said elsewhere, 'Joy is the seri-ous business of Heaven.'"[9]

Taken from:
The Screwtape Letters
C. S. Lewis

---

9. C.S. Lewis, *The Screwtape Letters*. (Old Tappan, N.J.: Fleming H. Revell Co., Lord and King Associates, 1976), p. 172.

"I shall know why—when time is over
And I have ceased to wonder why
Christ will explain each separate anguish
In the fair schoolroom of the sky.

He will tell me what 'Peter' promised
and I—for wonder at his woe—
I shall forget the drop to anguish
That scalds me now—that scalds me now!"[10]

Emily Dickinson

---

10. Robert N. Linscott, Selected Poems & Letters of Emily Dickinson. (Doubleday Anchor Books, Garden City, N.Y: Doubleday & Co., 1959), p. 67.

The harvest is past, the summer is ended, and we are not saved.

Jeremiah 8:20 KJV

Reality

"Very well then, atheism is too simple. And I will tell you another view that is also too simple. It is the view I call Christianity-and-water, the view which simply says there is a good God in Heaven and everything is all right—leaving out all the difficult and terrible doctrines about sin and hell and the devil, and the redemption. Both of these are boys' philosophies."[11]

Taken from:
Mere Christianity
C. S. Lewis

11. C.S. Lewis, *Mere Christianity*. (New York, N.Y: Macmillan Publ., 1952), p. 46. From **Mere Christianity** by C.S. Lewis, Harper Collins Publishers, Hammersmith, London.

Euripides

"Theseus: Amen for my woes! I have suffered calamity, great
beyond all ills overpass!
O foot of fate,
How hast thou heavily trampled me and mine,
Unlooked-for blight from some avenging fiend—
Nay, but destruction that blasteth my life for evermore
On a sea of disaster I look, on a sea without a shore,
So vast, that never can I swim thereout,
Nor ride the surge of this calamity.
What word can I speak unto thee? How name, dear wife,
The doom that on thee hath descended and crushed thy life?
Like a bird hast thou fleeted from mine hands,
And with swift leap hast rushed to Hades' halls
Never sorrow of sorrows was like unto mine.
On mine head have I gathered the load
Of the far-off sins of an ancient line;
And this is the vengeance of God."[12]

Euripides' Theseus

Taken from:
Hippolytus

---

12. C.A. Robinson, Jr. editor, *Anthology of Greek Drama, Hippolytus,
Euripides.* (New York, N.Y: Holt, Rinehart & Winston, Inc. 1949),
p. 208.

"I saw in the night visions, and, behold, one like the Son of man came with the clouds of heaven, and came to the Ancient of days, and they brought him near before him."

Daniel 7:13 KJV

"For, behold, the day cometh, that shall burn as an oven; and all the proud, yea, and all that do wickedly, shall be stubble; and the day that cometh shall burn them up, saith the Lord of hosts, that it shall leave them neither root nor branch."

Malachi 4:1 KJV

What Time Is It Really?

The Lord swore He would never again destroy the earth with a flood. Scripture points to fire, and not rain, as an agent of God to alert. The second chapter of Peter, verses 10-11 gives us something to think about.

The Meaning of Words

Peace through strength. Winning a nuclear war. Global village. Radicals. Opponents. Liberals. Conservatives. Right-wing. Left-wing. Bible-belters. Pro-choice. Cautiously optimistic?

What do these words really mean, and what do they imply? Are they an adequate label of some group's particular philosophy, and/or are they used to try and represent (falsely or accurately) a certain attitude and stereotype reflected by the context and degree to which they are used?

I quote an author, who I believe, has some significant insight into the use of words in our society. The following is a quote from Franky Schaeffer's book, *A Time for Anger: The Myth of Neutrality.*[13]

"Our world is deeply deceitful. The 'liberal,' humanistic elements of American society do not play by the rules they espouse: the rules of open-mindedness, fairplay, and equality under the law. Deceit and evil always go hand-in-hand, and our own age finds them wedded once more. For example, think of the abuse of language today. 'Choice' has come to mean death. 'Government assistance,' control of the population. 'Liberal,' an indefinite tolerance of everyone and anything, except those who disagree about issues on the

---

13.   Franky Schaeffer, *A Time For Anger: The Myth of Neutrality.* (Westchester, IL: Crossway Books, 1982), p. 15.

basis of moral principle. 'Pluralism' no longer means that men may differ in their views of truth, but that truth does not really exist, outside the limited spheres of science."

"The media's posture of neutrality can hardly be maintained when it transforms the news into *theatre which it produces.* The media's growing mania for power and their discrimination against Christians and traditional Judeo-Christian ethics only represent one portion of their current deception."[14]

"As long as the Christian only sets out to convert souls, fine. But let him stand up and begin to challenge the dominant, humanistic forces and the press will make every attempt to either ignore or ravage that individual."[15]

The prayers of Jesus (John 17) reveal to us that without the power of the Holy Spirit in the truth of Jesus, the Church would be ineffective to do much good as a whole, let alone stand strong. It is only because the Lord Jesus sent His spirit, that His Church *can* be a light in a dark world.

14. Schaeffer, A Time For Anger, pp. 41-42.
15. Schaeffer, A Time For Anger, p. 28.

Solzhenitsyn

Page 21

"On the other hand, destructive and irresponsible freedom has been granted boundless space. Society has turned out to have scarce defense against the abyss of human decadence, for example the misuse of liberty and moral violence against young people, such as motion pictures full of pornography, crime and horror. This is all considered to be part of freedom and to be counterbalanced, in theory, by the young people's right not to look and not to accept. Life organized legalistically has thus shown its inability to defend itself against the corrosion of evil."[16]

"This tilt of freedom toward evil has come about gradually, but it evidently stems from a humanistic and benevolent concept according to which man—the master of this world—does not bear any evil within himself, and all the defects of life are caused by misguided social systems, which must therefore be corrected."

Page 23

"The press, too, of course, enjoys the widest freedom. (He uses the word 'press' to refer to media also.) But what use does it make of it? Here again, the overriding concern is not to infringe the letter of the law. There is no true moral responsibility for distortion or dis-proportion. What sort of

---

16. Assorted quotes from **A World Split Apart: Commencement Address Delivered at Harvard University** by Aleksandr I. Solzhenitsyn. Copyright (c) 1978 by the Russian Social Fund for Persecuted Persons and Their Families. English-language translation copyright (c) 1978 by Harper & Row, Publishers, Inc. Reprinted by permission of Harper Collins Publishers, Inc.

responsibility does a journalist or newspaper have to the leadership or to history?"

Page 51

"The West has finally achieved the rights of man, and even to excess, but man's sense of responsibility to God and society has grown dimmer and dimmer."

Page 51

"If, as claimed by humans, men were born only to be happy, he would not be born to die. Since his body is doomed to death, his task on earth must be more spiritual. Not a total engrossment in everyday life, not the search for the best way to obtain material goods and then their carefree consumption. It has to be the fulfillment of a permanent, earnest duty so that one's life journey may become above all an experience of moral growth: to leave life a better human being than one started it."

Page 59

"If the world has not approached its end, it has reached a major watershed in history, equal in importance to the turn from the Middle Ages to the Renaissance. It will demand from us a spiritual blaze: we shall have to rise to a new height of vision, to a new level of life, where our physical nature will not be cursed, as in the Middle Ages, but even more importantly, our spiritual being will not be trampled upon, as in the Modern Era. This ascension is similar to climbing onto the next anthropological stage. No one on earth has any other way left but upward."

Taken from:
A World Split Apart
Aleksandr I. Solzhenitsyn

False Gods

A country of divination.   Leviticus 9:31
Isaiah 8:19-21
Deuteronomy 18:10 NIV

"O time thou must untangle this, not I; it is too hard a knot for me to untie."

Shakespeare's Viola
Twelfth Night
Act II, Scene II

"Nor need we despair to be living at a time when we have lost an Empire on which the sun never set, and acquired a Commonwealth on which it never rises. It is in the breakdown of power that we may discern its true nature, and when power seems strong and firm that we are most liable to be taken in and suppose it can really be used to enhance human freedom and well-being, forgetful that Jesus is the prophet of the loser's not the victor's camp, and proclaimed that the first will be last, that the weak are the strong, and the fools, the wise. Let us, then, as Christians rejoice that we see around us on every hand the decay of the institutions and instruments of power; intimations of empires falling to pieces, money in total disarray, dictators and parliamentarians alike nonplussed by the confusion and conflicts which encompass them. For it is precisely when every earthly hope has been explored and found wanting, when every possibility of help from earthly sources has been sought and is not forthcoming, when every recourse this world offers, moral as well as material, has been explored to no effect, when in the shivering cold the last faggot has been thrown on the fire and in the gathering darkness every glimmer of light has finally flickered out—it is then that Christ's hand reaches out, sure and firm, that Christ's words bring their inexpressible comfort, that his light shines brightest, abolishing the darkness forever. So, finding in everything only deception and

nothingness, the soul is constrained to have recourse
to God himself and to rest content with him."[17]

Taken from:
Malcolm Muggeridge
Christ and the Media

---

17. Malcolm Muggeridge, *Christ and the Media*. (Grace Rapids, MI:
Wm. B. Eerdmans Publishing Co. 1977), p. 77.

Chapter 4

Sowing and Reaping

"By dividing body and soul, we divide both from all else. We thus condemn ourselves to a loneliness for which the only compensation is violence—against other creatures, against the earth, against ourselves. For no matter the distinctions we draw between body and soul, body and earth, ourselves and others—the connections, the dependencies, the identities remain. And so we fail to contain or control our violence. It gets loose. Though there are categories of violence, or so we think, there are no categories of victims. Violence against one is ultimately violence against all. The willingness to abuse other bodies is the willingness to abuse one's own. To damage the earth is to damage your children. To despise the ground is to despise its fruit; To despise the fruit is to despise its eaters. The wholeness of health is broken by despite."[1]

Wendell Berry
The Unsettling of America:
Culture & Agriculture

---

1. Berry, *The Unsettling of America*, p. 106.

I saw the earth, lo chaos primeval, the heavens, their light was gone. I saw the mountains and lo, they were quaking and all the hills rocked to and fro. I looked and behold no human was there. The birds in the skies had all flown. I looked and behold the tilled land was desert, its cities all lying in ruins from Yaweh, before His fierce anger. This is what Yaweh has said, "A waste shall the whole land be though I will make no full end. For this let the earth lament and let the heavens above don mourning, for I have spoken and not relented, I have purposed and will not turn back."

Jeremiah 4:23-28 KJV

In the Book of Jeremiah, the prophet speaks "The harvest is past, the summer is ended, and we are not saved." The prophets of God today speak as clearly as they did in Old Testament days. God will not turn back on His word. The earth is soon to reach her end, and the Book of Revelation draws a sharp sword to all those who say "All is well in the land," for the final showdown between mammon and the Spirit of God will be a cataclysmic confrontation with nuclear weaponry being used as God's judgment tools! To deny this is to delete the Word of God. The prophets tell us the "whole earth will be consumed by fire" which the breath and nostrils of mighty God will unleash on an unbelieving, unrepenting generation.

The spokesmen today, God's ministry to the churches (apostles, prophets, pastors, teachers, and evangelists), are often heeding the words of man rather than the voice of the Holy Spirit. We hear so well that "all is well between us and God," and yet *"all is not well in the land"* when the horn has not been raised and the trumpet blast has not gone off in our spirits to call us into a place of fasting and praying before our Lord, for as we know, judgment begins in the house of Israel first.

It was a high school theology class. Fr. Joe taught the class, and I still remember the wall plaque he gave me at the end of the 12th grade school year. It said, "Time is a tree—this life one leaf—but love is the sky." Whenever I have moved over the years, it is still in the box of things I pull out and say to myself, "I should throw this out, I really have no use for it," but I don't. These are words which remind me that God was watching me before I ever knew Him.

Funny what you remember about your school days. I couldn't wait for seventh period class to be over so I could go home, but I liked this teacher who gave me the gift. I remember that he had a ruddy complexion (really an acne problem), and the kids in class used to make fun of him. He was a godly man, a kind priest, sensitive and compassionate, and definitely a decade or so ahead of his time. I remember there was a gentleness about him, and I always wondered what it was that I liked about him.

When it happened to me years later, I knew why he was different. He had the Holy Spirit! He definitely was ahead of his time. He was walking on eternity's gravity, and carnal man walks on his own time. A big difference! There always seemed to be a deep river running through him, and I didn't know what it was about him that seemed to know things about us we didn't know. I know now that he walked with God (as Enoch did). The God of the Ages lived underneath that too over-starched collar he wore. He told me to live life well, and to find meaning and purpose for my life. Every 17-year-old needs a sage to guide him or her. Searching for truth has been playing 'hide' and I playing 'seek' until I found the buried treasure, my soul in God's life.

Hope Is the Diamond That Surfaces
Amidst the Pile of Ashes

Avoiding a commitment to Christ is making self the savior. Think of what the world says—Don't put all your eggs in one basket. Think of what Christ says—I AM your all in all. What a difference.

It never dawns on you all at once—but over a period of time when you begin to realize that your prayers are not answered in the way, shape or form that you thought they were going to be. There is nothing like a good dose of reality to burst your idealistic bubble, and there is nothing like the smell of hope to let you know that there is no aroma that will wake up your soul like courage.

I was lying in bed one night, and the Scripture flashed into my mind "suddenly the King in all glory will come to His temple." I realized that we are His temple. I realized that answered prayers are the manifestation of the Son of God *that* works in our lives. That Scripture is as real as the physical manifestation that will take place when the King of kings and Lord of lords stands in His holy temple. The temple building now is alive with flesh and blood; His people are His dwelling place.

Just as the curtain of the temple was rent in two, the flesh and soul (where His Word pierces between) are rent when the Lord visits His temple. There will be occasions where our flesh is broken open and we die (in Him, the flesh death) and He'll pour in—as He fills us with new wine, His precious anointing.

My spirit will sigh a deep moan of relief when my heart is laying on Jesus' chest. My reward will be Him holding me! Only then we will know what every day and hour and our very lives meant to Him when He has us in His arms and is holding us.

On Busting the Enemy's Chops with the Savior's Punch

What is the nature of a bully? To tease, harass, intimidate. Street gangs deal with bullies all the time. Bullies are people who want to steal fruit from a tree they never planted. That's what satan tries to do to Christians who profess their faith in Jesus Christ and who claim the Word of God over their lives. I once heard a preacher testify that he and his wife have already claimed God's will for their kids' lives (their little kids were all toddlers). They both came from broken homes. When they both got saved and gave their lives to Jesus, they were determined that the enemy was not going to rob their kids' lives the way that he had robbed their young lives. Years and years of wasted time could be unwasted if only we gave Jesus the rights He already owns. Ownership: 9/10 of the law. I always loved God and had a heart for Him, yet my ways were rebellious and stubborn; and even now, I wrestle with an awareness that He wants control of ALL MY LIFE.

Real Nursery Rhymes

"Somebody's been sleeping in my bed," said the baby bear. "And somebody has been sleeping in my bed," said the momma bear.

I used to wake up for school, and there were two bedrooms I had to pass down the hallway before I made it to the hallway bathroom. I like waking up slowly and getting into the day. I was never a jump and up and at 'em type of person. I stretch like a cat and come out of my dreams slowly, often knowing the answer to my prayers the night before are lying somewhere between my sleep and waking. When I oversleep, it messes up the ease of that. When I make a mad dash out of the house for work, I never quite feel like I started the day right. Often, ol' sleepy eyes would wake up as a kid and mosey on down to bed number one (which my sister occupied when she wasn't in the bathroom putting on mom's makeup at 7:30 a.m.). Then when they'd call, "Lizzy, you can go in the bathroom now," I'd wait until my brother saw it was unoccupied and then I'd have five more minutes of sleep. Finally, when everyone was at the breakfast table, dressed and ready for school, I would be making a mad dash to brush my teeth and comb my hair (which I still can do at the same time—and quite nicely), tie my shoes and pull up socks at the same time.

WHY? Because those first five minutes when you wake up are so precious to me, and I didn't want to lose them. Also, the beds were already warm and it was a good feeling to lay there snuggling until the cold tap water called my attention at 7:00 am.

The first five minutes of waking are the best for me. When Jesus gets a hold of our spirits and wakes us up, the best time is when the morning light floods our spirits with untapped treasures and hidden manna of how good life is, and how wonderful it was of God to include us in it.

Kids' Korner

Be humble or you'll stumble
Be careful or you'll fall
Don't forget it's God who gets
the glory for it all!

There is a lighthouse not far from man's sight
He's CHRIST the lightbeacon, the hope for us all
No respecter of persons is Jesus the Son
He rides the ship of salvation for the lost and the hungry
He is the only anchor, He's the one.

There's a juice that runs in every living soul
it bubbles and it runs when Jesus takes control
talking to the neighbors is sharing His lovely light
makes the lonely feel so loved when their world is made
alright."

Original Songs

Remnant of Jehovah

Chorus: I am a remnant of Jehovah, I am a remnant for my God
the Lord Christ lives within, I am a remnant for my God

"I am a daughter for Abraham, I am the sister to St. Paul
by faith am I in covenant with the Lord who made us all.

Chorus

I have been made ready for the harvest, made ready for the King
My bridal gown is clean and white, Come Lord, enter in,

Chorus

His outpouring, His anointing is open to us all
There's nothing Jesus Christ can't do, with a soul who gives his all."

Chorus

Jesus Is the Son of God (sung to army marching beat)

"Jesus is the Son of God, the Living Word, a mighty rod
He saved my soul on Calvary, His blood plunged me to victory
Alleluia, Allelu, see oh see what God can do
Alleluia, Allelu, see oh see what God can do."

Royalty

Chorus: I am a member of the royal family, the bloodline of Jesus
Christ. With kings, and queens, and princes, He has made the bride His
wife. He has made us all His wife....

"With royal bands of glory, and honor from the throne
He has called together the nations, and made our hearts His home
He has made our hearts His home.

The temple will soon be ascending, from souls just filled with praise
He will shout the 'trump' of victory, He will raise us to life without end
We will be transformed as His face we gaze, we will see His face—and be changed."

Chorus

There's a Pot Brewing on the Stove

There's a brewing that has been going on in me for some time. Read Psalm 86 and you'll see that although our life often brews tribulation as well as joy—although we may have "been laying among the pots" (the Scripture writer was referring to the people of Israel when they were in slavery), there is a silver lining for the church—Her Redemption is in Messiah.

Sometimes it feels like suspended animation between the time prayers are prayed and answered. The lingering stretches of time almost make us feel like the ant who had been stepped on yet didn't die, just walking dizzily and half alive to make it to the other side of the road.

Buried Treasure

The Gift That Gives Three Times Back

The greatest gift a woman can give the man she loves is respect. Respect is like a silk linen that is folded on three sides. The main fold is the fold of love, turned over by the fold of joy... Humility is the final fold that binds the sides of respect to form a three-fold pattern. (As the Word of God says, a three-fold cord is not easily broken. When the Father, Son and Holy Spirit agree with you, who on earth can take it from you?)

When God opens our eyes and we behold His glory, we see how truly humble and full of mercy He really is. When God wins our heart by His love for us, we become changed, glory to glory, every time we encounter His love.

Do You Know What You're Saying?

When someone says to a woman who just lost a child, "Oh, be glad you have three other children," you wonder, does she really know what she is saying? People who grieve need listeners who understand that delivery is often more articulate than content, especially in matters of the heart. Imagine a friend saying to a friend who lost an arm in an auto accident, "Well, gee, you still have one arm left." This is true—you still have one arm left—or three children at home—but that doesn't negate the loss and the emptiness that exists for what is lost.

As a friend who had lost a child was telling me that she couldn't handle the pain of the loss (without His grace), the Lord reminded me that even with all the nations on the earth and multitudes of children playing—His heart still grieves and longs for one nation that is lost. God is still grieving and longing for Israel's redemption—the way an abandoned husband, who still loves his wife even after she has left him, still longs for her to come back to him.

No amount of anything else will do—God wants HER back. And God has a unique way of retrieving what is His. If only we would learn to cooperate with the Spirit of God, generations of pain would be avoided. The human way takes so much longer. Even in loss we are grateful for what we have, but that doesn't mean we shouldn't acknowledge our loss. Not dwelling on it—or being in a prison of grief so that you can't live the future—but to deny or say loss doesn't matter—is to nullify the value of the one who was taken. When people would say, "Be glad you're single," I used to feel it was like saying to a starving woman who desired children, "Be glad you're in a famine—just think, no dishes to do."

It's all relative—your soul, your hunger, God's heart, God's hunger for the nations.

Experience Gives Compassion

Ever notice how pat answers apply until you're confronted with the same situation you gave a pat answer for—and it doesn't work! You want results, you want your prayers answered—you need answers yesterday. Suddenly, you realize, fear is someone else's problem until you have no job, mounting bills, sick kids, and have to figure out how to feed five kids. Times like these make you realize the Lord giveth, the Lord taketh, and nothing is eternal in *this* world's system. It's all a gift—nothing we've earned or even deserved—but a gift from God.

Your brain's a gift. Your health is a gift. Your arms are a gift. Your spouse is a gift; your heritage, your children are a gift. Life isn't a business, it's a journey. No one fills out a purchase order three months before he is born and orders parts or makes requisitions for talents. It's all given. It is only when you're hungry, or hurting, or needy, or being stretched to the limits by God, that you can appreciate this.

I have found out people generally don't want pity when they hurt. They talk to justify their own emptiness, as if sharing the need will validate their own existence. Prayer is just that; it validates our creation. It makes us aware we are created—not Creator. It gives identity and purpose to every single solitary soul. This is why I believe the greatest tragedy of communism (even in the horrors of starvation, abuse and tyranny) was to abandon God. When the "state" is made God, one is asking for misery. Ever read Dostoevski or Aleksandr Solzhenitsyn? To make it a crime to pray is to crush any man's or nation's identity.

Justification by Blood

The only justification that will stand, at the end of the ages, as I stand before my Maker is the blood of Jesus Christ. No other word, event, action, or thought will do—at that moment. Only His blood will justify my life. My choices. My actions. My words. All of it will be summed up as the Lamb opens the Book of Life and sees (your name): Saved, Delivered, Justified.

Awards stay here on the walls next to your diplomas. Even if you were to be buried with them, where we go we don't need them. Heaven has its own reward system—read the Book of Revelation. In heaven, it is God who will reward with a soul-winners crown those whose lives were a witness to others to become disciples of Christ. There are those whose faithfulness and perseverance revealed Christs' power and holiness in their lives. These saints will shine forever and ever—and Christs' joy will satisfy the soul. Can a plaque on earth satisfy your soul the way it will when Christ hands you one?

How did our names get in the Book of Life? Certainly not by our power, strength or good works. If Christ were to judge us by penalty and we were to see all our sins written down, who could stand? It's mercy that judges you even when you have judged yourself. The writers of the New Testament knew this when they said to judge themselves. Examine your own consciences. If you allow God's fire to try you here, it is a fire you can live through—no matter how hot the flames. Remember Daniel in the lions' den? Trust will carry you. But to be in the fire whose flames never go out—this is too horrible to know.

God intended no one to enter hell. Think of time—for a minute. Christ every minute, every hour, every day, every month, every year. Multiply how many minutes in your lifetime (you didn't know it was that high, did you?) you have lived so far. Do you mean that in all these minutes you can't say a prayer that takes only one minute: "Lord Jesus, I repent. Come into my life, let me live for you"?

Corporate successes and top managers hire people to prove the productivity that can be accomplished in a span of time—minutes, hours, days, weeks, months. Think what can happen to your soul if you give just a portion, a tenth, of what belongs to God back to Him. He only wants your time because He has you in mind. He loves you, and He knows spending time with Him helps you. He doesn't need the help.

The Voice of the Lamb

"God sings to the ages, if only you'll hear, the prophets are within us, He is close and very near.

To anything that touches, the resemblance of a man, I saw the Father swooping out of Heaven, that large but graceful hand.

I saw Elijah dancing, ah, He always loved a jig, Malachi was swaying, He conducts old prophets' bands.

Don't think it's time that measures the distance of the sun, its ebbs and wanes and waxing moments. He's the unveiled God, revealed in the Son. Poems aren't words wasted on sheets of yellow and white, they're history and prophecy, unwrapping our dullness so we can see.

There's so little time to make the measures of your song. Know the tune and hear her tempo, days are being shortened, and where will you go, where will you go, after He comes, only a few days left to watch the setting sun..."

L.M.

Highway 81

Coming up highway 81, the rain finally gave way to a break of the sun. It was all I could do not to cry for some passion. In God's time, love brings His deep, holy action. Driving with tears flooding my lap, turned the car off, then I drove, then I sat. Pulled the car over and turned the engine off. Thought I heard ol' Gabriel blow, been hearing some sounds you don't normally hear, the sounds not the audible kind, but for our spiritual ears. Dreams are just about over for this page of earth's life, so few hear the trumpet, they figure staying alive is enough of a fight...who has the time to listen to trumpets anyway....

The music of the Father is the orchestrated ALL, He is sending HIS SON to catch earth before she falls. The SON has a rhythm, sounds like liquid gold, if you could only catch the beat, before you get too old. Wined and dined by silver, wrapped in pearly white, is the wooing of His spirit, He really makes you feel alright.... Next time you feel a swaying, moving your soul to sing, next time you feel like dancing, you know you got the beat, give way to loud notes crying, like wailing in the wind, you're on your way to higher ground, the net's soon dropping, my friend, and Gabriel, he'll swoop you in.

Sing loud and break the sound of space, you're really redeemed, oh human race, rip open your naked shameful face, the angels are walking toward us with grace, emeralds and pearls on HIS glove, He's cupping a rose He picked just for me, The Savior has put His purple cloak around me. Don't call me scarlet, I won't answer by that name, Call me the living, my former days are all under the sea. The Sea, the sea, God almighty has put little old me, under the sea, sins and all, under the sea. I am no more what I used to be, I am a new woman, a bride to see, The only thing fairer than the noonday SON, is the wave that's rolling toward us, and written on it, is THE LOVE OF THE SON, THE LOVE OF THE SON, HIS BRIDE IS HIS LADY, earth and heaven, now made one.

The Rock That Won't Be Moved

Alicia, did you really expect a response from these old friends with whom you used to live and work? I mean, you moved, and they heard about your mom's sickness and struggle with Alzheimers, but did you expect them to be there for you? Well, I guess I had hoped they would. The Word says, "Love believes all things, hopes all things, trust all things." I guess I thought because I was there for them years ago, they'd be here for me when I needed them. "You know," said Peg, "if you go through enough in life you learn that your Rock is really the Lord. He is the only One who will always stick closer than a brother. I mean, look at Job's friends. It was easy to speculate why all these terrible maladies were befalling him as long as they were Job's maladies, but when they hit too close to home, forget it. I think it was really neat when the Lord said to Job, you pray and then I will heal your friends. God vindicated Job's suffering and testing by saying to him, if you pray for them, then I will heal them. It was easy to judge Job until they were stricken."

Remember when God got fed up with Israel. He was ready to wipe them out and work with Moses. Yet, the humility and mercy of Moses (whose heart was well known to God) interceded, and God spared the nation.

I was the listening ear as I walked along the mountain road with my two old friends that day. Suffice it to say, we had all been through the "fire" in our own lives, particularly in the last several years.

I broke in on the conversation and said, "You know, what will people do when things get really rough? I mean, faith is the testing ground and measuring rod we all go through to some degree or another." I reflected on how I as a new believer would always sing, *Lord, mold me, make me, break me*, yet when He does, oh boy. We always sing songs of repentance at churches, yet when its our turn—do we stand?

I have learned you don't give pat answers. Every life is unique. God might call one woman to stay, travail, and intercede, and another to leave for a better land. God knows people's hearts—who will change, who won't. I truly believe difficult situations require personal direction from God; you can't play God for people.

As Shirley wisely said after church one Sunday, "Liz, don't people believe the prophet who speaks judgment has first been judged by God? God makes sure you understand the territory. I mean, if He has put a message of repentance in your soul, you can be assured God has spent nights and weeks and years birthing it in your spirit."

Travail for answered prayer is harder than any (natural) birth, I believe.

Moses never asked to be Moses—God made him Moses. Joseph never asked to be in the prison—but he was. Abraham and Sarah didn't want to wait 90 years—but they did. Paul was a mighty instrument of God and prayed that his pain would be taken—but it was not.

How can we judge these saints until God has put us through the same ordeal?

Shirley and I went for coffee. She looked me straight in the eye and said, "For the first time in my life, I can understand why Christians lose hope and sometimes faint. Not that

I am contemplating it; there is a fierce perseverance in me to stand and endure this season of testing. Why?" "Grace," I said.

At least I have been honest with God. Shirley said, "Liz, our lives are not alike, but circumstances were designed by God to work out what He wanted to work in our lives. I guess when the Word tells us to put on the garments of praise, God engineers even apparent loss to bring victory."(1)

The prophet in Jesus made Him a man well-acquainted with sorrow. The prophetic ear to hear the Father and know wisdom gave Him such clear insight that it brought pain. Wisdom will bring both pain and joy in this life because knowing and understanding bring purification. Purification is painful because it is always the truth. Truth is like a miner panning for gold: when you shake the tin plate, there is nothing left but gold.

Denominations won't do it. Your church committees won't do it. If you are trying to find God and His will, be willing to be poured out like water. When a sword pierced the side of Christ, know it also pierced the church. The husband and the bride are one—one spirit—and what one feels the other feels. If you are being pierced now—look up—your redemption draweth nigh.

The natural tendency is to turn from the pain. I know. But run into it. Christ wants us to. Let every dream and hope die, what resurrects will be life. When the seed falls to the ground and dies, it bears fruit. Let all your dreams and hopes and illusions about the good life die. The way I see it, we all have a choice: we can do it God's way or our way, and disobedience is very costly. I hope we learn to listen to God's first trump, than to wait till His last call. There is a fire coming on the world, and those who do not yield will not be ready when the Lord returns. When a season of testing comes, it burns up all that is not of Christ, not born of the Spirit. Can your faith stand the test? If we do not understand these words now, what will be in the days to come?

Chapter 5

The Earth Is the Lord's and the Fullness Thereof

Genesis chapter 20 speaks of the first male to open the womb as being holy to the Lord. The good book also tells us that Jesus descended into the bowels of the earth and then ascended into heaven. In God's plan, He purposed one Son, Jesus, begotten in His image, and many adopted sons and daughters to be destined for His image.

In His Image

There are more parallels in heaven and earth than we could dream. Over two-thirds of the earth is covered with water, and a little over two-thirds of our human bodies are comprised of water fluids as well. Earth's topography is comprised of over 70 percent water, and this percentage applies to human beings as well. Our creator does all things perfectly. Ever hear of Mandel's Law? It is a scientific principle of genetics which supports that life units occur in pairs that separate during gamut formation, even in the smallest cell stage of life—there we are two by two—side by side. This is also called the law of dominance. Just goes to show Noah wasn't the only one pairing them off, two by two. Remember what God told Noah and his sons—fill the earth and subdue it. There it is again—that law of dominance. The strain of life is ultimately stronger than the fiber of death. There is a symbiotic pattern in the basic components of all life matter, and there is no more separating the heavens from the earth or the sun from the moon than there is the spirit from the soul. To respect one is to know the other.

Power of Sounds

Sounds have an enormous power; specifically, it is words that have the greatest power to affect a human life. Words can change your life. A simple "I love you," at the right time, has the power to heal, deliver, set free, encourage, strengthen and much more. Conversely, words of hate and fear (all insecurity comes from fear) can cripple, destroy, tear down and pronounce death to the soul. Perhaps all who dwell in heaven best understand the power that is wielded by the tongue.

If your life was a sound, what would roll off your tongue? Sweet music? A clear, crisp melody, or a grating shrill? It all depends on the words you choose and how you choose the tone you say it. I believe children are imprinted and molded by eight years of age from what they see, of course, as well as what they hear. Choose sounds that make your children grow healthy in soul. Teach them what love sounds like.

Hide and Go Seek

Ah yes, we all have "buried treasure" somewhere. You might stumble across it when you walk alone. You might run into it in a house full of kids, but it is there, always there, lying among the tossed clothes and dirty dishes. The Holy Spirit often hides Himself best in imagination, so don't be afraid to dream; you can never exhaust God by hoping too hard. (See 2 Corinthians 4-7.)

"To dare to live alone is the rarest courage, since there are many who would rather meet their bitterest enemy in the field, than their own hearts in the closet."—Colton

Understanding—and the Fear of God

It doesn't take a rocket scientist to figure out that the countries are run by either men of prudence and wisdom or "Humpty Dumpties" who are about to have a great fall. The lust for power always pillages a nation, and no people suffer more than those who have a leader without wisdom or understanding.

Job 12:23-25 could as well be talking about a number of this earth's rulers today. History tells it as it is, for when a man governs who spills the blood of his own people to display the arrogance of his own pride and folly, you can be sure this ruler is not listening to heaven. Folly groomed him for such a day because without mercy and understanding no one can rule wisely, yet alone compassionately. The greatest sign of integrity in leadership is the appropriate use of power. True authority (governmental, spiritual, et. al.) is a burden. Authority is not an honor to be sought; it is an obligation to be fulfilled.

Remember the lessons of the Old Testament's kings, especially Solomon. He asked God for wisdom and got more than anyone before or after him; yet time would prove that even wisdom, with undisciplined passions and the mixture of grace with sin, would spell ruin. Solomon's ruins were not limited to the temples he built; he ended up far differently than he started out.

To discern the times in which we live (1 Chron. 12:32), we need to understand what the Word of God and the Spirit of Truth can teach. It is important, extremely important, to pray according to the Word of God, as Ezekiel did, as Esther did, as Deborah did, as David did, as Jesus did, to pray God's will for nations and peoples. To "pray for those in authority over you" ensures mercy from those who govern far more decidedly than to believe every electoral promise you hear as "gospel." What is gospel is to ask God to give leaders godly wisdom and understanding. What is gospel to ask God to give leaders a fear and a love of God. How can anyone lead a nation, or serve a nation in righteousness, unless they can submit to a higher authority themselves? If they have no fear of God, what makes you think they will respect you?

It is sad to see what is happening in the Middle East or in Eastern bloc countries when people have only had idols. These statues have given the people the only thing they know: a dead god and a leader who has hell in his heart. Give these nations the gospel of Christ and watch what happens. When Jesus stated that "nation would rise against nation," He knew that the battles that would be waged against His Kingdom would be spiritual, not just physical adversity. Our Savior assured us that just as He overcame the world, the destiny for His Church is victory if we walk in the light. The truth of our salvation is the freedom of Christ's life in us. Those who have tasted freedom die for it, rather than be a prisoner. As it is with nations and peoples, so it is to those who have tasted freedom in the King of kings and Lord of lords.

Peace with God

Old-timers often use the expression, "Yea, ol' Harry made his peace with the Maker before he passed on." Peace with God is simply making peace with Jesus Christ, as He is our peace. Since no one comes to the Father except through Jesus Christ, it is good to get to know the One who opens the pearly gates—well in advance of your arrival there.

Strange Irony

The greater one's ability to suffer, the greater is one's ability to understand. To be able to discern and ponder is proportionate to the ability to absorb wisdom, and there is no painless way to put the soul in abeyance while the mind is still learning. And this is one of those "mysteries" we were told about as a child that one day we would understand.

An Aria That Only the Heavens Can Sing

It is one of those rare nights that the television has an Italian Opera on—and a good one at that. Richard Wagner's "The Ring" is playing, and I can hear the heartbeat of another prophetic song, the kind the spirit of God writes.

From my perspective, the opera foreshadowed the relationship of Lord Jesus Christ to His church. Brunnhilde was the sleeping maiden who left her god-like state as she was kissed by a human prince and awakened. She now becomes fully human—she sees her love—the prince (young lad Siegfried). At first Siegfried thinks the sleeping one a man, yet discovers her to be a woman. "Awake, be a woman to me. Arise from darkness. I am part of you, if you love me. I am wise only because I love you. I see and feel only you. I awake after a long sleep. Who is this hero who awakened me? My sleep has ended. I have looked into your eyes and I am blessed. You have restored me to life. You were dear to me ever before I saw you." Brunnhilde even sings, "I greet you son, I greet you light, I greet you radiant day." The young man sings *"In the fire I shall find my bride. Now I'll call to my beloved."* ("In the furnace of much affliction, I have chosen you behold.", or "I am my beloved and my beloved is mine"). When the words, "Is the helmet pressing on the hero's brow?" were sung, I thought of the helmet of salvation we now wear which Christ appropriated for us. I thought of the armor of Christ (see Eph. 6:10-18). When the hero sings of his sleeping love, "How can I awaken the maiden, to see her eyes open?", was this author aware he captured the Song of Solomon, the prince called Christ and His Church for an opera? The best love story is still the story of Christ and His bride, no matter how often it is penned or in what form it takes.

Pearls

To the one who made all the jewels and gems in the earth, the adornment most stunning on a lovely neck must be a garland of grace and a string of mercies. What can be stunning to God except that which is worn inside and reflected by the soul?

The Image or the Essence

One particular Sunday morning, as I was having break-fast by myself, I felt myself tearing up as the Lord reminded me I needed to deal with something. The Lord reminded me of a friend I needed to forgive, as He began to speak to my heart about fears we both have. "But Lord, what do you mean she is more afraid of me than I am of her? She intimi-dates me. I mean, after all, she makes five times what I make, has a husband, three kids, and a nice home, and she is a tough cookie if you step on the wrong toe. She is not as vulnerable as I am. She's tough!" Oh, how God loves to teach us.

Michelle is an old co-worker from way back. I had reason to phone her this morning concerning an unfinished project from long ago; and once again, I got off the phone feeling like a total failure. Oh, she is always very nice—that's just it—she's nice. She seldom lets down the gates to the castle of her soul long enough to let you look in. Every conversation winds up the way a short chat with the man who you won't buy insurance from ends—courtesy—a nice, professional, "thank you, Ma'am"—just socially nice. Yet, we had worked and laughed together, and for no explained reason, she be-came a fortress unto herself. Naturally, my third grade teacher's remarks came back to haunt me. "Well, you must have done SOMETHING wrong, Missy. After all, if Sally Ann won't play with you at recess, you must have done something wrong." The devil always hits below the belt, you know. The 'father of lies' plays dirty, always hitting your mind with a blow from the past that SHOULD long ago have been washed in that great sea of "forget it" and "it's over and done with." (You know, it was some twenty years later at a department store that I ran into the now married Sally Ann, found out her parents split that year, and that she was too afraid to trust anyone. I didn't know that *then*; all I knew was if something went wrong, was it my fault?)

We go through life feeling overly responsible for that which we should have no qualms for, and not paying enough attention to the needs of those who should get our utmost. All this until we learn to get it right. I am still in school on the lessons of life, but as I drove to Mickey D's for a Mc- "feeling lousy about myself today" breakfast, I realized I could not go to church and face God until I first faced the enemy within.

Why does her non-acceptance of me, her rejection of me, bother me so? What have I done to warrant her suspicion, Lord, or worse, her feigned politeness, which is obviously forced when we speak. I had many an inferiority complex around this woman, and all I ever wanted her to say was, "Hey, we're not perfect yet." I mean, we are both Christians, and nothing is worse for brethren than feigned "like." Healthy truth, and that in doses of reality, can be much more palatable than emotional dishonesty. Few things can cause confusion and unrest (the very things Christ came to deliver us all from) more than emotional dishonesty. Fact is, no one was ever meant to be everyone's friend or like everyone (I might like brisket, you might like pork), but we can love each other in His name. Truth is, I have found out praying for those who you know don't accept you will give you an understanding of them far more than you would know, and it is impossible to sacrifice for someone without starting to care for them. And it is a sacrifice to the flesh to pray for those "who treat us ugly" or as the Scriptures say "persecute you."

And I poured out to the Lord, just why does He so often put me in situations like this, to face rejection (and no soul feels more self-justified than when it is unjustly rejected, or perceives it to be so)? As always, He patiently listened. He said nothing to my heart, but I am sure He was thinking plenty.

It was an hour later at church I would hear Him respond to my questions. Even now, as an hour ago, as I took a shower to clean my skin, His Word was washing my mind and He said, "Liz, people always expect an image. They want things to be so; and when they are not, they are uncomfortable. They are threatened. You threatened her, as she perceived it, even though in reality it was not the case at all. She envied your freedom; and in getting close to you to trust you, she had to look at her own self.

There are things in her life I am causing her to deal with now that she doesn't want to face. Your presence there made her uncomfortable. She couldn't figure you out, and because you didn't fit the norm of what she expected, she shrugged you as rejected by Me. We both know that is a total lie. You were the substance in flesh, of what I created you to be when I designed your pattern, and she is the substance, not the image, of what I designed her to be. She is having a hard time accepting her life, and things are not for her as she thought they were 'supposed to be.'

So, Liz, will you love her for Me? I know she hurt you, but will you rise above it and just love her for Me? Forgive her the way I forgive you all the time for your faults and misgivings. Will you show her that I am a God for all flesh and have no favorites? Remember Liz, I went to the cross rejected and despised for you. I forgive you seventy times seven because I love you. Eternally. And nothing in heaven or earth or under the earth can ever change My love for all My children. Will you love her despite your own self?" Well friends, how can you say anything after that?

As always, after God speaks, our speeches to the Lord (like Job) fall to the ground in embarrassment. All the while, I thought she didn't like me and her rejection of me in the time we worked together was because of something wrong in me or about me. And all along, I was just the salt that got too close to the open wound. Why is it, we take rejection so personally? Why is it, we sometimes forget (or at least I know I do) that Christ Himself was thought to be "despised by God" by those who thought they knew God well? Why is it Christ became rejection because He never tried to be anything more than what He was? He was called a glutton and a winebibber. He hung out with "real people." He loved the polished and learned, unpolished and unlearned, fat and small, and tall and short all because He refused to be more concerned with IMAGES than the SUBSTANCE. Yet, unlike me, He ALWAYS rose above the situation, and sinned not. He always was in touch with the Father; so whole, His emotional state was never in a tizzy as mine has been.

You know, knowing God, or being "saved" doesn't make you immune from life's hurts. In fact, you're twice as likely to feel rejection or loss in a more keen sense—as you're twice as vulnerable to life and its inhabitants.

Oh yes, at church, the pastor spoke on doubt as being many things: apprehension, uncertainty, fear, disbelief, you know, all the lies the enemy tries to cause you to believe about yourself when you feel so rotten. As he spoke in detail on the nature of doubt, I was wondering if I was blushing in my seat—you know, talk about conviction. He also spoke on forgiveness: the sermon you don't want to hear when you want to be mad at someone! I always thought I had a lot of faith, and most times, when your faith isn't tested, you do. But when you've been in the fiery trials for a while and they all kind of run together, well, doubt can come upon you like an unexpected tidal wave, and you either swim or sink. I'm a good swimmer, yet lately my arms are getting tired. But grace will strengthen me again, she always does.

The Mind of God

How did Jesus know to fast 40 days in the desert? Divine revelation. How could He discern the hearts of people? Divine revelation. How did He know the cross was the Father's will for Him, that He had to suffer for the sins of the world? Divine revelation. So why should the Church today not believe God works in like fashion?

If the Church is given "the mind of Christ, let this same mind be in you" (Rom. 12:2), is it strange that we should know things ahead of time? Is it strange that God should prepare us for events in our lives? You know, some of the most difficult testings of my life (and I admit I did not pass all the tests) came as a result of knowing some things before the fact, if you will. What an awful beating I took trying to carry it in my OWN UNDERSTANDING. I mean, without His grace and rest, we can't carry a thing.

How foolish of us to judge each other when we don't know all the facts. I mean, as Hannah told me, two months before her mom died of a sudden illness with emergency complications, her mom was in good health, so everyone thought. She "thought" she heard the Lord tell her to pray for her mom and be there for her, that the Lord was taking her "home soon." Fortunately, her mom knew the Lord, yet it was hard to know this. I mean, you certainly don't tell your family, especially if they aren't believers, and you just kind of pray a lot and ask God all the time "Was that really you God?" for no one wants to be deceived. The Lord says He is the good shepherd and HIS SHEEP KNOW HIS VOICE. If He wants to communicate something to you to prepare you for a specific event or such, He will, and you will KNOW it is Him. God created us in such a way to know Him by His Word, His Spirit, and His Presence in our lives.

God is God, and He can do anything He wants. Should He decide to trust you more than you know you would trust yourself, know it is because He loves you enough to carry your cross. There will be times that discretion and discernment will tell you to keep your mouth shut. God speaks some things for you to pray on, shut in with Him. There will be times you might beg God for someone to trust, and He will provide you a friend as an island. Most of all, anything God says is a truth. There is no sin in truth. It might require (no, *it will require*) patience, long-suffering and waiting on God to the zenith, till you see the fruit of what He has spoken over and over to your soul; but you have no choice. Should your little hands try to "make it happen," it will never be as right as when He is in it with you.

Real maturity and love is the ability to give love, forget whether it's reciprocated or not; it's the truest measure of a soul's greatness. The ability to love unconditionally is what makes a mortal soul divine.

Dominus Vobiscum

You know how it is. You'll be driving to work and hear a song on the radio, and a phrase or memory from childhood runs across the street of your mind like a child darting out from behind a car. Hey, where did that come from? Like the day Dominus Vobiscum came to mind as I saw a procession televised on TV. As a kid, when the Mass was in Latin, I could remember "The Lord be with you." I wanted that. Didn't really know Latin, but I knew I wanted Him with me, always, even until the end of time, just like He promised. I even remember asking Him, on days I felt particularly vulnerable, or days when I felt I had not made the mark, "Will you still really always be with me?" Even as adults, we have trouble understanding unconditional love.

He will never leave us or forsake us. Do you really understand what *never* means? Capesh? Comprende? He will never forget us. GLORIA A DIOS FOR HE TRULY IS WORTHY. As Sister what-was-her-name said in Catechism, "Why were you made, class?" "We were made to love and serve God." They sure put education in the right order, for it is easy to serve someone after they have been loving you a long time. OK class, listen up, "Why were you made, world?" Answer: To love and serve your God. A+! Now you can skip limbo and go right to heaven (Hmmm...I think that is what He was planning to do all along...I mean, where did limbo come from, anyway?).

"And the Comforter, Whom I Will Send..."

Jesus Himself said it, "And the Comforter, whom I will send, He will tell you of things to come." Hear it? He will tell you of things to come. The Spirit tells us He wants to reveal. Revelation: the KEY to the KINGDOM. What Jesus said to Peter He would build His church upon, and the gates of hell wouldn't prevail against it, is divine revelation. The voice of God directing our lives.

Selective Memory

I heard someone's grandmother say they can remember the flavor of the first ice cream cone they ate at the sweet shop 60 years ago, but they can't remember where they put their support-stockings yesterday. What marvelous selectivity the human brain has that it makes its own little seaways, of sorts, to automatically file people from events, times from places, important data from trivia.

I think the appeal of "brain" game shows is part of the wonder of stored information in a vault most of us will never see. The hardest working and most faithful servants in the universe are your cerebral cortex and medulla oblongata. Boy, would Vanna have fun turning those letters! God made us wonderfully, the psalmist proclaimed. We facilitate the knowledge of people in a more intense way than facts. We remember people, events and words in a singular way. Are we being equipped for eternity, when we "will have the mind of Christ" (and know and see past realms for space and time)? What a dimension of glory for those who live in the City of God.

I can remember walking home from kindergarten, and the class brat stepping on the heels of my shoes till my feet ached and I cried coming in the kitchen door. "Mom!" (I wanted to punch his lights out, and when I told the priest at church, he told me to forgive him, ignore it.) Hmmm. It would take me some twenty years to learn how to correctly understand anger and action and appropriate responses. Whether age five or 50, we all need to learn to deal directly with timed responses.

I remember the look on the gas station attendant's face when Gloria and I dressed up as Groucho Marx and a Cinderella princess (I didn't look as good in a mustache as she) and asked for a full tank. The 50-ish man laughed and said, "Oh, I get it. A costume party." Nope. We dress like this every night; we're going home to dinner and the kids." We laughed all the way back. No special reason. It was a Friday night and we were bored and wanted to dress up the night with a few laughs.

I remember hundreds of minutia, most of it insignificant, some of it very funny, some of it sad, some of it just plain life. Yet, if you asked me where I put my barrettes I just took out of my hair an hour ago, I'd have to do a hunt and search to find them. Why is it we can't find our car keys when it's time to go, but we can always find room to remember the things that shouldn't be so easily remembered, like criticism and negative words?

I want to live long enough to befriend my cerebellum. I want to tell my good stories when I'm in my eighties. I figure if I'm a friend to my memories now, while I'm making them, they'll be gracious to me when I'm old. When I start wearing my shoes without socks, or butter my toast on the wrong side, I'll need friends like that.

It would seem that Adam and Enoch and all their lineage were pretty spry and sharp men—and Israel had good eyesight—even in their 90's. Maybe there is real hope for this generation.

The Treasure of Darkness

The treasure of darkness is that it makes the light more beautiful, and it silhouettes reality with hope. Years ago when the astronauts first landed on the moon, and then spent that wondrous journey traveling back to earth, I wonder how they must have felt. They were a part of this, the living, part of the world creation, and saw it from a perspective few could appreciate.

When Christ visits a soul with a "born-again" experience, or when His spirit touches a soul with the revelation of Himself, everything, even the world, seems momentarily suspended in time, like a state of sixth grace. How wonderful are those rare moments where we sense God's wonder in an unusual way. We feel a harmony, a sense of oneness and purpose in life's daily activities, and sense the joy of being part of God's plan. No darkness or worry can erase the joy of the light of Christ which is being revealed in us. A child can take joy for granted, because he has known little else. When Christ is in us, the hope of glory is revealed, even the ordinary events can seem spectacular. If the child is blessed with a happy childhood, a small toddler will relish the morning, tumble out of his bed and into yours, and lap up the day like a puppy waiting to be petted. How many adults have retained that sense of life well into their middle years?

If everyone who has ever thought of giving up, or even those who contemplate ending it all, could come out of the darkness for just a moment and look at the world as that first astronaut saw it, they would never be the same. Since few of us will ever get to travel to the moon, a similar and more viable means of transportation is the Holy Spirit. Without the revelation of God's presence in my life, giving me joy, I could not make it.

As Ralph used to say to Alice in the Honeymooners, "to the moon, Alice, to the moon." Ralph, I can do one better than that; "to the stars, baby, to the stars. That is where we're destined. All because we believe!"

You Are the Potter

I had a six-week break inbetween semesters and needed some credits, so I took a sculpting course, of all things. College is really one of those few times in your life that you are not all entangled with responsibilities and such. I often said if someone would pay for it I'd go to school, a course or two a year, until I can no longer read.

It was an interesting mix of lives in the classroom. A banker working on an MBA wanted a "fluff" course to relax to, a housewife needed some personal kudos, and a random mixture of ages, colors and backgrounds were all present. We were given the clay, some instructions, and had patterns to work from. We were to sculpt a variety of projects. Well, the figure I was working on for some reason seemed to take on a shape of its own. We did painting and sculpting, and the student next to me graciously said my paintings seemed like an abstract Cezanne. Interesting, but what does that mean? My "real friends" told me I shouldn't consider a career in painting. When I asked where the painting was that I gave to my friend, and it was on the floor in her garage so her puppy could use it as a place mat for nibbles and bits, well, I wasn't offended. I mean, it was not a Monet, but at least it was functional.

Yet, the sculpting, that amazed me. I tried deliberately in the three weeks of the clay molding process to make a certain type of figure, and this piece seemed determined to be something else. When it was finished, it was not the bust of a historical figure or the outline of a body (as we were to try and achieve) yet it was a man's face. I remembered thinking; this face looks familiar. If you ever saw the replica of the Shroud of Turin, you would remember the vague, sketch outline of a face. Well, this face looked like Christ's face, and I couldn't understand how that happened. Even the woman next to me said, "You know, it looks like one of those faces you would see on a holy card." (Do they still have those?) It was the only thing I did not discard from that class. I took it home, and until it got moldy and had to be laid to rest in the kitchen disposal, it reminded me how Christ can do all things through the clay, when we understand it is He alone who is the Potter.

I am no sculptor, and if I tried to repeat that figure again, I probably couldn't. But I did learn that when the anointing of God rests on one of God's children, whether for a moment, a minute, an hour or a season, there is no music that can't be composed, no art that can't be created, no war (spiritual) that can't be won, and God alone gets the glory. The Lord has a wonderful way of bringing humility to bear on a situation: if you tried to do it on your own, without the anointing, it could never be done.

Chapter 6

She Is the Dream

As both sexes reflect the image of their Creator, I wonder what dreams and hopes were in God's heart when He created the female species. It is interesting that when God decided to make women, He first put Adam to sleep and from Adam's needs and God's hands, woman was made. From His side was she brought forth. It should be obvious there was more on God's heart than Adam; there was woman. He made them both IN HIS IMAGE.

At its best, the church is neither male nor female; but one in the spirit. Just as God the Father is above the earth, whom He husbands, the first Adam was to till the ground and tend to and take care of Eve. I have known few marriages where there was real joy when this was out of order. One protects and provides, one nurtures and sustains. One is the dream, the other the action. One whispers ballads, one shouts marching songs. One fights with tears and intercession, one fights with arms and strength.

There is no real difference in the imagination of God. Just as the Church is His dream, borne of His desires, the Church is His desire just as the wedding is the culmination of the desire to couple. One is the dream. A woman who knows her God is as close to a dream that walks that a husband can know.

In Revelation 2:7 and 22:2, the Scriptures refer to tree of life which bears life giving fruit for the healing of the nations. Even as God ordained the human seed from our fathers to work the miracle of life in our mothers womb, we can believe even the natural process of biology, down to the biologic cycles of woman, is patterned from a greater cycle. Before time began, God had planned that from Jesus would come all *spiritual seed*; Jesus who hung on a tree, becomes our *tree of life* for all the cycles and times and months of man. Such a holy gift bears the process for humanity to bring forth glory from clay. There is nothing unholy about what God has dreamed. Blessed is the man who has a wife who knows who she is in Christ, and how blessed is He who receives this wife as the living dream she is: he receives favor from the Lord.

We Have This Treasure in Earthen Vessels

"No one can buy it, and no one can hold it, no man can claim it as his own. The best he can do, if he wants to be true, is to relish its scent and the rapture he's known. Like time in a vacuum, He stands alone, and no one can measure the faces He's known.

Just like the glory of the God we've never seen, the best you will do, is to treasure His dream. Learn from wisdom that time is a gift, a borrowed gift, that stands as a testimony to the glory of life.

If you learn to love time and what it can do, you'll find that time will someday befriend you. Mercy is made of this, and the elements of time and wisdom find a favored soul on a journey that has no end."

To His Glory

"I became the flower for the picking at Your hand
You're the garden-master so come and dress me in Your love
And clothe me with Your silver touch
And take me in with crimson strands to the Promised Land.

I can no more live without Your Spirit, than I can live without
Your new wine.
Your love became my future when You came into my life
I really need to know Your peace as you take me through the
night.

God's requited lovers really have a better end
They get the best the Master has, when they embrace their
destiny's end."

The Princess Tale

"You brought me flowers
I sang You my song
You gave me promises
I held all the night long.

You called me tender
and said if only I could see
The passion, the desire, that
You've always had for me.

You told me that wars were fought for love stories like ours
You even slayed the dragon to hold me in Your arms.

You touched and kissed and wrapped me in the power of
Your love
You said I was Your dream, Your princess sent from heaven
above.

You called me Your beauty, when my warts I did see
You even wiped my tears away when You saw me bowed low
beneath the tree.

You told me to write so eternity would remember well Your
Son
as a Lover and a Savior and a Redeemer all in one.

Oh Father, Dear Father, my Holy Creator
these are my only flowers that I have to offer Thee.

You called me Your princess, as I protested with sighs
How could a poor girl like me be the apple of Your eye?

Royalty, You declared, is the statement of the soul
for when you're birthed from heaven, your lineage is always
noble."

Life Really is for the Birds

It was on my way to work today while waiting at a very long stoplight that I noticed a flock of birds to my left, circling above. The unity that they flew with and the gorgeous patterns they made as they flew overhead were something to see. Yet what determination to get that one piece of bread that was on the ground. If only the church would be more like these tiny beauties. They have unity and grace, yet they always get their meal, God's provision, no matter what. They fly all over for one piece of bread without breaking rhythm, leaving the flight pattern, or getting off base. They fly in perfect harmony as they were meant to. We, the Church, have the Bread of Life within us. We should be able to keep up with the birds.

Best of Both Worlds

Science has long recognized that people who predominantly use the right side of their brain are given to an intuitive way of looking at life. The ability to discern times and events with visionary perspective has graced poets' words and prophets' hearts throughout man's history. God can use an artist's hand to reveal the spectacular glory of creation. He can inspire dreamers and thinkers to effect humanity's good. It takes far greater courage to dream than one would imagine; a dream is just an unrealized potential, for oneself or the world.

The left hemisphere of the brain often controls the reasoning process, and accounts for the logical and analytical mind. Often, men were thought to be the left-lobed species, and the open emotions of women made us look like a right-lobed bunch. The truth lies somewhere in the middle. Without reason and common sense, the world would be in a state of chaos. And without the right-lobed souls, this ordered world would be too devoid of joy and hope.

Since man is made in the image of God, I suppose God's glory reflects the best of both worlds. With His supreme intelligence there is nothing He does not know. He created all things, foreknew all things, destined all things, does all things. With His heart and soul, He loves all things, has mercy on all things, fashions all things, takes pleasure in all things. The perfect symbiosis of the two worlds (or hemispheres), heaven and planet earth, is Jesus Christ. Christ lived in perfect wisdom and knowledge (brilliance, left-lobe) and had perfect understanding and discernment (right lobe). The gifts of the Holy Spirit and the human reasonings were able to marry in a perfect soul, a soul devoid of sin. This is the legacy of the Church. When all believers will one day be "like Him," we will be perfect without sin. The marriage of His spirit with ours makes for a glorified soul, a perfect vessel. As Jesus said, let's not waste our time pouring new wine into old wineskins. Getting closer to perfection means aligning yourself to your Creator. Once you're with Him, the "new" everything comes with the territory.

Take courage—if you've always been a left-lobed soul trying to break free from tradition. Live and experience life rather than organize it, analyze it, and strategize it. Remember, there is room on the high wire act for another one. Faith is like a high-wire act—it's a jump of courage into the unknown but oh, such a wonderful trip. You'll never be sorry you jumped into the water, but you will long regret never trying. And for the right-lobed souls who find that following patterns and established conventions make for a peaceful life, it is better than chasing the wind.

Covenant Promise

I think it was the winter of '81 or '82, that two friends and I went to a church for a "healing service" we heard so much about. It was reported God used this priest in unique ways, so Mike, Karen, and I got in the car and left. After a very anointed healing service, there were only the three of us and this priest in the church. Some people close up bars, we close up churches. Somehow we were the 'last call' group for those who hadn't received prayer. That really isn't so bad when you consider the Word says, "the last shall be first" (Mk. 10:31).

I remember walking up to the priest as he was gathering up his Bible and mentioning how blessed I was by his message that evening. With that, he took my hand and started to walk me over to the altar steps and knelt down along side of me. I could feel my heart thumping inside my chest. What is this man doing I thought? He then stood up over me and took my left hand, touched my ring finger, and said "the bride." He said, "the bride of Christ." He then prayed in a language I didn't then understand (the gift of tongues), said a few more things to me, blessed me, then said "Good night" and walked away.

As I stood up and started to walk to the back of the church where my friends were speaking, I remember thinking, "What did he mean, the bride?" As we walked out the door and made our way to the car, Mike and Karen asked, "Well, what did he say?" When I told them, Karen said, "Oh, Lizzy, oh my, this must mean you're gonna be a nun. The Lord must want you for the convent life." I sobbed all the way home.

The last thing in the world I wanted to hear was that I would spend the rest of my life wearing black. I was meant to be a nun like cows were meant to fly. Yet this word: it was as if I had been "chosen" to be banished to a solitary island of one. This wasn't the word I had hoped to receive from my Lord.

It was but a few years when I understood that the Church is prophetically spoken of as "the bride." I understood that the Lord meant I was part of the redeemed, that divine heritage that the "remnant" or "called out" ones are to the Church. My friends and I can have a laugh when I think of how I *first* heard that word. When you don't understand a prophetic word, you can't receive (with faith and peace) what the Spirit wants to give. There is no greater gift for the "bride" than to understand in her heart the word of her Lord and Master. No—He didn't want a nun—but a daughter.

Counting the Cost

"I was too busy learning, so I haven't been earning the gold you think I should have.

Met too many saints, caught under the weight, do you know He sends laughter as healing salve?

Tears by the buckets have sewn in my soul what even the books cannot tell.

You cannot walk with the Son and be welcomed by the wind unless you drink deeply from the well within.

The highway to holiness is traveled by few, for who wants to walk that way.

You travel alone, there is no other way, the Savior can etch Himself in you.

You'll wake with His face, carved into your soul, and in loving life's broken ones, the Savior Himself carves you totally whole.

You cannot explain, the riddle that offends, to those who have no ear to hear.

You do the best that you can, as He holds your right hand and gives you grace for the promised land.

The soul of man, can never understand, unless it's been fanned by the winnowing hand. A hand that prunes, and tests, and tries by fire, your very soul, till there's nothing but gold to melt in the fire.

Spinning straw into gold is not a tale that only children sing, for the day is approaching upon chariots of fire when we'll both be carried into the presence of eternity's King.

Where do you stand as time gives the final command? Are you ready to sing, in the presence of the King as His voice RINGS out into all the land?

A lifetime of trying to hear the Spirit's sighing has caused me to hear with tears in my ears.

I hear the earth's groaning, her temperature is soaring, she is ready to be rid of her disease.

All maladies of souls, with perplexities, she's groaned, her barren womb is being made clean.

You can't understand, unless He's taken your hand, the Song of the Spirit which makes you free."

The Restraint of the Lord

The Lord exchanges His strength for our weakness, and the longer I live I see how much restraint and long suffering He endures for His Church. It has been said that you never really get to know someone until you have lived with them. If this is true, who knows us better than the only one who is with us morning, noon and night, but the Lord. The Lord knows when we're gracious, and when we turn away from His grace. He knows when we're leaning on His strong arm, and when we're trusting in the arm of the flesh. All in all, you will find out if you haven't yet, that no one will always be faithful or perfect in His love to you, except God. He is the romance of my soul; He allows me to be the romance novelist I always had within me and He allows me to express it freely. He allows me to be that when I need to be. He graciously accepts whatever you can give; He isn't insulted by one single stem rose and He isn't impressed by millions. He looks for gardens, but if they're not in your heart, you haven't really tasted His life yet.

He-Man of the Universe

He makes even the small ones warriors, and He puts words and faith into their hands so they can bring down kingdoms of darkness. Ever hear a small child say, "Daddy, what is heaven like?" He makes even the small to regard Him, and the faith of just one soul can do great things. I know of a wonderful actor who needed Christ more than he knew. It wasn't the preaching of great orators that brought him into the Kingdom; it was his small child who was battling with illness, who was curious about God and life and heaven. I marvel at how God uses the tender things to break through walls. God knows how to reach us, doesn't He?

No one alive, except God in the flesh, could fulfill all of the Law of God. The Holy Spirit was sent by God to give us the rest and the victory in knowing we need not live condemned by the law: it is fulfilled in Christ's holy blood at Calvary. Our hope is secure in knowing Jesus Christ passed every test and completed every good work that the Father ordained for Him. The good news is that we (the Church) are the gift and present to God Himself, bought by Our Lord. It is a marriage contract that should make you commit, but it is the love and the desire for the lasting joy of love to continue that should make that contract a pleasure, not a duty. I always brought the man flowers when I dated. I needed romance more than him—and the first man to bring me flowers was Christ. The first One to give before it was given was He who brought me into the light of day, and He has not stopped giving lavishly. Mercy, time unlimited to His counsel whenever needed, He is always there. When you realize your lover and best friend is also the husband of your soul, you'll realize only God can be all things to all people. If my husband on earth loves me but with a tenth of His love for me, if he loves me enough to bring me flowers, he'll have more love back than he can hold. That's the way love is; when it is not meted out in spoondrops in the giving, it is doubled in portion in the receiving. Husband, get ready for a lifetime of joy. I have been with the Lord, and I am more than ready to give to you.

Chapter 7

The Prayers of Abraham, Issac and Jacob Are Being Answered Today

Mercy Rejoiceth Over Judgment (James 2:13)

The mighty one of Israel is coming back to be revealed in a people who survive the sword of darkness (see Jer. 25:29) that covers the whole land. The Father God has never stopped loving His wife Israel, nor has His Son given up on His bride, the Church. God has a plan for His people. When Jews and Gentiles, the seed of Isaac and Ishmael, Jacob and Esau, Arab and Jew, embrace (even out of need for survival) in the *hope of the Messiah to come and save them*—then the Lion of Judah will raise His head and His glory will be seen in the land.

"... 'The people who survive the sword will find favor in the desert; I will come to give rest to Israel'" (Jer. 31:2 NIV). Have you been wearied coming through the dry places of life? Be assured—you will be watered with refreshing. Israel has been thirsty for centuries—she is due for her latter rain. She will be watered.

"See, I will send you the prophet Elijah (the spirit that "prepares the way for the Lord" is the voice of the army of God—clearing way the high places and thorny ground) before that great and dreadful day that the Lord comes. He will turn the hearts of the fathers to the children, and the hearts of the children to their fathers, or else I will come and smite the land with a curse. (Malachi 4:5-6 NIV)."

Isaiah 59:19 and Revelation 12 reveal that the enemy will try to destroy the man-child, but is not victorious. The Lord Himself rescues His bride and her children: the people of faith. Only in the arm of the Lord are we safe.

Restoration of the Soul

If pride goeth before the fall, then presumption runs before humiliation. In the course of our faith, the occasions will arise (when you least expect it) where you will be at a test and not be aware that you are being tested. Let me tell you about a dream I had. In 1990 I dreamed that I was in a classroom, sitting at my desk, taking a test. I knew that this was a very important test that I was taking. I had a sense that I was being watched by three—standing above me. I heard the Lord say to me that I was being tested. When I woke up, I looked up every Scripture I could find in my Bible concordance on "testing." I made a note, in my heart, to be aware so that I could pass this test. I did not know that the "test" that the Lord gives is when we don't expect it, nor in the mode we expect it.

In the next two years, up till now, there have been times that I experienced a wave of depression like I never have before. (The battle for our soul is in the mind). Every promise God had ever given me seemed more remote than ever. It is as if the enemy comes to us and says, "Hath God said?" every time we hear from heaven. Every word is a prophetic word from the Lord, be it Rhema, Logos, or spoken by the Holy Spirit through a human vessel. The word that the Lord gives us, after His seed enters our heart (by faith), is much like the growing of a tree. The more enduring the word, the more possibility for fruit—to that end it is as if every circumstance blows across our path to try and speak otherwise.

There were several times the last year I found myself identifying more and more with Peter, the one who was so confident he would not deny Jesus. Thank goodness God looks at our hearts and knows and tries us. Like Peter, I loved the Lord, but began to see more and more how He had to bring me to the end of myself. More than once I found myself awake on my bed, wishing things had been different and telling Him so. My heart loved Him, but the soul needed to be broken, even more. We all think we trust God fully, until the last vestiges of everything we hold dear is held weighing in the balance. In moments of crisis, the loneliness of the dark night of the soul, and the fanged tooth of our adversary that tries to devour the Word that He puts in our life—in moments like these, we see the nakedness of ourselves, and our need to rely on Him. Like Peter, we give our good ideas and opinions to the Lord, only to find that the pattern, over and over, is one of abandonment to the divine schematic, a brokenness beyond anything we've ever known (if we are to reach the hundred-fold anyway).

When we deny the Lord, we deny the Father, we deny the Son and we deny the Holy Spirit. When we hurt the Father, we hurt the Son; when we hurt the Son, we hurt the Spirit.

In the natural course of adulthood, we remember our youth and can see decisions based more on zeal than wisdom. In things of the spirit, without the meshing of both, we can never grow to mature sons and daughters. Deliver me Lord, from myself. I want to look like the "after" image of the before-and-after shot of Peter's soul.

"The quality of mercy is not strained, it falleth as the gentle dew from heaven."

"Portia"
William Shakespeare
The Merchant of Venice
Act IV, Scene I

"For the Lord your God is a merciful God"... Deuteronomy 4:31a NIV
"Has God forgotten to be merciful?"...Psalm 77:9a NIV
"...'for I am merciful,' declares the Lord"...Jeremiah 3:12b NIV
"Blessed are the merciful"...Matthew 5:7a

Untapped mercy. The most necessary principle to untapped mercy is that you must be willing to be stretched. Pride quickly goes out the door in an hour of need. Stretched beyond yourself, your own reasoning, your own ability, your own self, is the life of the Church: grace. Grace can stretch us beyond anything we can perceive. To achieve a desired end, your vision must be greater than yourself. Your hope must exceed your limitations, or you can never enter your promised land.

God has purposed a walk of faith in Christ Jesus for all who acknowledge Him as Lord. The road that you walk may be different from mine in the paths you choose or the circumstances you encounter, yet all who know Jesus as Lord will learn that the Good Shepherd will lead us all to a place where victory in our lives can only come through obedience to His will and word in our lives. Christ is the pattern for our redemption, in that the Holy Spirit will use everything and anything on the road that we walk on, to make us and mold us to the nature of Christ.

His pattern is one of stretching: it can never be avoided. At some point in your life, if not many, you'll see only by the power of the cross can the aroma of Christ come out of you.

His pattern is one of purpose: He can and does use everything in our lives to achieve good ("And we know that all things work together for good to them that love God, to them who are the called according to His purpose." Rom. 8:28) I have found it necessary to know those words as life. It is what gives the grace to endure the testings and tribulations that will come. This is Scripture. You will soon see that grace is needed more than you know.

Who is a Rock Besides Our God?

Understanding etches her resolve into you and the testing builds discernment: once you've been taken apart, brick by brick, to have your foundation rebuilt, you become a house that can stand. God takes you apart so He can put you back together again His Way. When the walls that are built are built on any material not of Him, you cannot withstand the hurricanes and the floods, the tornadoes and the earthquakes. Unless the "living" material cements your stone together, you will look like little more than Jericho's wall which came tumbling down. We need to look to the city whose builder and maker is God. A fortress and a higher tower is the Lord of hosts. The stone that was rejected has become the chief cornerstone—and His Name is Jesus. The Church has been promised a *pure white* stone (Rev. 2:17), and this pure and white rock is Jesus Himself. This living Rock of Ages has outrun time and even death, and He is the final reward.

Faith is Courage in Slow Motion

Be strong...and of courage...for the LAMB has overcome the world

- *To him who overcomes, I will give the right to eat from the tree of life, which is in the paradise of God.* (Rev. 2:7b NIV)

- *He who overcomes will not be hurt at all by the second death.* (Rev. 2:11b NIV)

- *To him who overcomes, I will give some of the hidden manna. I will also give him a white stone [new mind, new eyes to see] with a new name written on it [the name of the redeemed], known only to him who receives it* (Rev. 2:17 NIV). To all of God's children, He gives a priceless revelation of Himself that only a bridegroom can give to a bride. There is a special love—a tender romance—the song of the redeemed that only the blood-bought saints can sing.

- *To him who overcomes...*Revelation 2:26. [the millennial reign—the victory of Christ]

- *To him who overcomes...*Revelation 3:5 [salvation]

- *To him who overcomes...*Revelation 3:12 [part of the New Jerusalem—come down to earth. Part of the group which was written "the meek shall inherit the earth."]

- *To him who overcomes...*Revelation 3:21 [the eternal government of God—a part in His reign]

- *To him who overcomes* Revelation 21:7 [inherits all that is a part of the riches of God]

Faith Is Courage in Slow Motion

Be strong Church

- The hidden manna is that which is hidden; (revealed only by prophetic revelation), the inspiration and teaching of the Holy Spirit. When Jesus, who was full of joy in the Holy Spirit, said "I praise you Father, Lord of heaven and earth, *because you have hidden these things from the wise and learned, and revealed them to little children,* He was revealing the key to the Kingdom: revelation knowledge comes by trusting faith in God alone. Yes, Father, this was your good pleasure (Luke 10:21).

He Is My Strength and Song—and Has Become My Salvation

Exodus 15:2

I have waited for a child of promise. Years ago, I made a covenant to God to wait to marry the man that *He had for me* (and I have been tested in the wait). I got to the point in my life where I said I wouldn't date anymore (I hadn't for years). There's nothing wrong with it, you know, but I wanted the steak and potatoes—the real thing. I was a daughter of the King, from a royal household of faith (see Psalm 45). Why throw my heart (pearls) away on a stolen kiss? I knew (from my past) shortcuts don't satisfy—they only increase your anguish for God's way in all things. Leanness of soul was given to the Israelites because they were not satisfied to wait for honey in Canaan land. They had oodles of quail—but no happiness.

I wanted honey. I wanted to kiss the prince (husband) not just the flesh. I wanted, desperately, to kiss my future, to wrap my arms around my reward. I would settle for nothing less. I had gone through too much fire (of God) to disinherit my gift from heaven. I remember the story of Ishmael. Although God blessed him, and made a great nation out of him, he was not the promise (Isaac) God had intended. God intended to bring Abraham and the wife He gave him—together—to make a nation out of his loins. The loins of Abraham were a covenant of faith (hence the circumcision) and the holiness of generational heritage. (Circumcision was not to be an idol, only a sign of the tender mercies of God—how He loved His children—just as we believers are God's portion and heritage). God's inward parts must be full of emotion and His bowels must be full of love toward His own. He is the Father and begets sons and daughters. Abraham would taste a smidgen of the glory and privilege God saw in being the Father to many descendants.

I wanted to give my father a blessing—an everlasting one. Just as my Lord gave me a new name (see Rev. 2:17), I wanted to give my human father, Victor, a heritage that he could look down on from heaven and be blessed in his soul. I wanted to give a husband—the one God meant me for—a child born of desire, love, timing (God's), destiny, faith, and the hope of Christ. I wanted to give Him the best I could—a pledge of love. I wanted to give my child a heritage and a destiny: to be given life—to be given salvation—to be given a mother and father who loved him or her enough to wait for them to be born. I wanted an "Isaac" blessing in my life. I wanted God's will.

I can tell you, surely, this is the truth. Every prophetic promise God has given me has been tested and tried, and it often felt like death. Every word dies before it springs to life. Learning to die to the word so it can rise in Christ takes time. God will not allow any man to taste His promises from his own strength. Before He's done with you, you'll know it's Christ in you and the hope of His glory that will do this thing. I felt like death (hopeless) with each year that went by: promises—but no reality of the promise yet in my life. Each year that went by I had more and more compassion and understanding toward Abraham and Sarah, Job and Moses. These became lives I understood because of the crushing from the enemy, the disappointments, the travail, the impossible circumstances that came against the word God spoke to me.

In the last few years I have had to ask myself, over and over, the hardest questions of life. Would I love someone all over again who would reject me? Would I live in a strange city? Would I be willing to give up what I have to get less (in the natural) while I know I'm gaining by leaps in the spirit—because I'm obeying to go where His spirit tells me to? Would I lay down the successes that were there if only I made a left turn instead of the *right one*?

Knowing what God wants to do in no way alleviates the pain of the wait, yet this is His PATTERN and there is no other way. If you try to take by force, by flesh, by lust or by sin, you are playing the devil's game, and you cannot win the prize of heaven which is victory and honor in Jesus Christ. Having to wait and watch many seeds (words) die is perhaps the most necessary lesson I had to learn. Many times over the years I've learned to say, in faith, "Let God be true, and every man a liar. God does not repent—hath He not said it, will He not do it?"

I said it to encourage myself in the Lord. I said it loud enough for hell to hear. The Church will crush the serpent's head for God will have a Church who will know personal and corporate victory and God's words will not be mocked. Those who believe on God will not be put to shame.

Could I give up the thing I cherished most: the love that He himself promised me so many years ago? Would I be willing to remain single to serve Him, if He asked, give up the birthright to have children? These thoughts rarely left me.

When Miriam sang *The Song of Moses* (Ex. 15:2)—she sang a prophetic song for all who are predestined to know Christ: The Lord is my strength and song. Many generations after Miriam, we are at that time when the Church will also sing aloud a victory song (Rev. 15:3). Jesus is God Himself, and He overcame even his own flesh, as to be slain, so we could have an everlasting Name! 12,000 upon 12,000's around the throne sing Yes... *"eye hath not seen what God has prepared for those who love Him."*

WORTHY IS THE LAMB WHO WAS SLAIN TO RECEIVE ALL GLORY AND HONOR AND PRAISE... (Rev. 4:11)

A Line Worth Repeating

One of the best quotes I've read in a long time is attributed to Michael Barkun, a political scientist at the University of Syracuse. In TIME magazine's fall, 1992 issue (p. 8), Mr. Barkun is quoted: "The human mind abhors a vacuum." When I flipped through these pages, I remembered what Christ said about the "light" and "darkness" so many years ago. When the message of the gospel is to "be filled with the Holy Ghost", we (created beings) are reminded that where there is absence, there is emptiness.

Be it a secular voice or a spiritual voice, God can speak through all things to direct and declare, exhort and edify.

As the scientist stated, the human mind abhors a vacuum. I recall the apostle who was blinded by the light of Christ, encouraging anyone who would listen, to "put on the mind of Christ." There is no emptiness in the mind of Christ: His mind *is the future*. The One who told Moses *I AM THAT I AM* was stating His fullness right there for all creation. When there is no absence, no lack, no need, no darkness, what else is there but fullness? Omnipotence and all wisdom and glory are in the heart of God. The Holy Spirit of the Living God knows all things before they happen: all past, all present, and all future is hidden in Him. The many names of God (from El Shaddai, Jehovah Jireh, Yawheh Rohi, Yawheh Tsidkenoi), are but a few names of the One who needs nothing added to Him to be completed.

It is only the creation that needs to be completed (7), and perfected (8), and called to overcome (10). Our ultimate destiny is to be assembled around the throne (12). With trillions of cells, and much of the human mind's potential untapped, it is only reasonable to believe (faith) that the mind we are given in this lifetime has only begun to tap the light of the wisdom and understanding, "that shall be revealed in us," as the Scripture says. "The fear of the Lord is the beginning of wisdom," says the Good Book. It has taken science 2,000 years to see it on a computer to be able to believe it. The fear, awe, or wonder of our Creator is where you begin to see the reflected image of the glory hidden within us.

For those whose names are written in the Lamb's Book of Life, their destiny is to "ever increase in the knowledge of Christ." The illumination of the truths of all eternity, all time, all God are for those who believe. Should the most brilliant man that ever lived, be he scientist or sage, die unsaved, his learning, living, and loving stops; he has only eternal hauntings of pain, what could have been, the loss of it all. And to the simplest, unlearned (but trusting) soul, their everlasting portion, their everlasting heritage is everlasting growth: in mind (the mind of Christ) and in personhood ("we shall be like Him").

Take a minute and read from the Book of Revelation. It is worth your time. It is the difference between life and death, fullness and absence, wisdom and foolishness.

Chapter 8

Weeping
for the City

The Song of Death

"FAREWELL, thou fair day, thou green earth and ye skies,
    Now gay with the broad setting sun;
Farewell, loves and friendships, ye dear tender ties,
    Our race of existence is run!

Thou grim King of Terrors! Thou life's gloomy foe!
    Go, frighten the coward and slave;
Go, teach them to tremble, fell tyrant! But know
    No terrors has thou to brave!

Thou strik'st the dull peasant—he sinks in the dark,
    Nor saves e'ven the wreck of a name;
Thou strik'st the young here—a glorious mark;
    He falls in the blaze of his fame!
In the field of proud honour, our swords in our hands,
    Our king and our country to save;
while victory shines on life's ebbing sands,
    O who would not die with the brave?"[1]

(Dumfries, 1791)

Taken from:
Selections from Robert Burns

---

1.   Robert Burns, The Song of Death, *Selections From Robert Burns.* (New York, N.Y: E.P. Dutton & Co., Dumfries 1791), p. 139. Edited by J. Hunter Craig, J.M. Dent & Sons, London.

Why do I count the clock that tells the time,
And see the brave day sunk in hideous night;
When I behold the violent past prime,
And sable curls all silver'd o'er with white;
When lofty trees I see barren of leaves,
Which erst from heat did I canopy the heard,
And summer's green all girded up in sheaves,
Borne on the bier with white and bristly beard,
Then of the beauty do I question make,
That thou among the wastes of time must go,
Since sweets and beauties do themselves forsake
And die as fast as they see others grow;
And nothing 'gainst Time's scythe can make defense
Save breed, to brave him when he takes thee hence.[2]

Taken from:
the *Sonnets* of
William Shakespeare

2.   William Aldis Wright, Cambridge edition text, *Complete Works of William Shakespeare*, (Garden City, N.Y.: Garden City Publishing, 1934), p. 1404.

You are the light of the world. A City set on a hill cannot be hidden.

Matthew 5:14 NIV

"Lo! Death has reared himself a throne
In a strange city lying alone
Far down within the dim West,
Where the good and the bad and the worst and the best
Have gone to their eternal rest
There shrines and palaces and towers
(Time-eaten towers that tremble not!)
Resemble nothing that is ours.
Around, by lifting winds forgot,
Resignedly beneath the sky
The melancholy waters lie."[3]

Taken from:
The City in the Sea
Edgar Allen Poe

---

3.   Edgar Allen Poe, The City in the Sea, *Oxford Book of Verse*, p. 208.

People will be lovers of themselves.
2 Timothy 3:2 NIV

"Man, introverted man, having crossed in passage
     and but a little with the nature of things
     this latter century
Has begot giants; but being taken up
Like a maniac with self-love and inward conflicts
     cannot manage his hybrids.
Being used to deal with edgeless dreams,
Now he's bred knives on nature turns them
     also inward: they have thirsty points though.
His mind forebodes his own destruction;
Actaeon who saw the goddess naked among
     leaves and his hounds tore him.
A little knowledge, a pebble from the shingle,
A drop from the oceans: who would have
dreamed this infinitely little too much?"[4]

"Science"
Robinson Jeffers

---

4.   Robinson, Jeffers, Science, *Oxford Book of Verse*, p. 783.

You will hear of wars and rumors of wars. Do not be alarmed. Such things are bound to happen, but that is not yet the end.

Matthew 24:6 New American Bible

The day of the Lord will come like a thief, and on that day the heavens will vanish with a roar; the elements will be destroyed by fire, and the earth and all its deeds will be made manifest.

2 Peter 3:10 NAB

"These grand and fatal movement toward death,
the grandeur of the mass
Makes pity a fool, the tearing pity
For the atoms of the mass, the persons, the
victims, makes it seem monstrous
To admire the tragic beauty they build.
It is beautiful as a river flowing or a slowly gathering
Glacier on a high mountain rock-face,
Bound to plow down a forest, or as a frost in November
the gold and flaming death-dance for leaves,
Or a girl in the night of her spent maidenhood,
bleeding and kissing.
I would burn my right hand in a slow fire
To change the future...I should do foolishly.
The beauty of modern man is not in the persons
but in the disastrous rhythm, the heavy and
mobile masses, the dance of the dream-led
masses down the dark mountain.[5]

"Rearmament"
Robinson Jeffers

---

5.   Robinson Jeffers, Rearmament, *Oxford Book of Verse*, p. 793. From **The Selected Poems of Robinson Jeffers** by Robinson Jeffers, Copyright 1935 © and renewed 1963 by Donnan and Garth Jeffers. Reprinted by permission of Random House, Inc.

Then I saw the beast and the kings of the earth, and the armies they had mustered to do battle with the One riding the horse, and with his army. The beast was captured along with the false prophet who performed in its presence the prodigies that led men astray, making them accept the mark of the beast and worship its image. Both were hurled down alive into the fiery pool of burning sulphur. The rest were slain by the sword which came out of the mouth of the One who rode the horse, and all the birds gorged themselves on the flesh of the slain.

Revelation 19:19-21 NAB

"In a dark time, the eye begins to see,
I meet my shadow in the deepening shade;
I hear my echo in the echoing wood—
A lord of nature weeping to a tree.
I live between the heron the wren,
Beasts of the hill and serpents of the den.

What's madness but nobility of the soul
At odds with circumstance? The day's on fire!
I know the purity of pure despair,
My shadow pinned against a sweating wall,
that place among the rocks—is it a cave,
Or winding path? The edge is what I have.

A steady storm of correspondences!
A night flowing with birds, a ragged moon,
And in broad day the midnight comes again!
A man goes far to find out what he is—
Death of the self in a long, tearless night,
All natural shapes blazing unnatural light.

Dark, dark my light, and darker my desire.
My soul, like some heat-maddened summer fly,
Keeps buzzing at the sill. Which I is I?
A fallen man, I climb out of my fear.
The mind enters itself, and God the mind,
And one is One, free in the tearing wind."[6]

"In a Dark Time"
Theodore Roethke

6.   Theodore Roethke, In a Dark Time, *The Norton Anthology*,
      p. 2272.

Then I saw new heavens and a new earth. The former heavens and the former earth had passed away, and the sea was no longer. I also saw a new Jerusalem, the holy city, coming down out of heaven from God, beautiful as a bride prepared to meet her husband. I heard a loud voice from the throne cry out: *"This is God's dwelling among men. He shall dwell with them and they shall be his people and he shall be their God who is always with them. He shall wipe every tear from their eyes, and there shall be no more death or mourning, crying out or pain, for the former world has passed away."*[7]

Revelation 21:1-4 NAB

7.   The Catholic Press. *The New American Bible.* (Chicago, Consolidated Book Publ., 1976).

"Deep in the greens of summer sings the lives
I've come to love. A vireo whets its bill.
The great day balances upon the leaves;
My ears still hear the bird when all is still;
My soul is still my soul, and still the Son, And knowing this,
I am yet undone.

Things without hands take hands: there is no choice—
Eternity's not easily come by.
When opposites come suddenly in place,
I teach my eyes to hear, my ears to see
How body from spirit slowly does unwind
Until we are pure spirit at the end."[8]

"Infirmity"
Theodore Roethke

8.   Theordore Roethke, Infirmity, *The Norton Anthology*, p. 2,273.

Chapter 9

Dreams

"In the depths of your hopes and desires lies your silent knowledge of the beyond; And like seeds dreaming beneath the snow your heart dreams of spring. *Trust the dreams,* for in them is the gate to eternity."[1]

Taken from:
Kahihl Gibran's
The Prophet

1. Gibran, Kahihl, *The Prophet.* (New York, N.Y: Alfred A. Knopf, 1923), p. 80.

**"I am pregnant with the seasons,
about to birth a summer child."**

This one thing I don't understand and that is why people don't listen to their dreams more. Do they not know it is in their subconscious mind that God is most at work? In peace, in slumber, the voice of the Lord is gently loud, strangely omniscient. I have awoken many times with a puzzle in my hands. All I needed to do was reflect on what the Lord was trying to show me, and the answer was quite clear. Not all dreams are so easily untangled. Yet one thing is clear. When a nation of people "have dreams and visions" of the end of the world, someone should listen to what the sleeping world is trying to tell us.

E. Mary Mickel

*   *   *   *   *   *

The Bible calls God's voice "a quiet, inner voice," the kind you hear only when you are at rest, or at peace with yourself. Before the millions run to catch their 6 a.m. train, or hit the car pools, or rush out the door, they could do themselves a favor by spending a quiet moment alone with God. He is not far away. He is as close as your soul. Remember, one morning and one evening comes quickly. As the Good Book says, "Seek the Lord while He may be found." The Lord does nothing in vain. If He has inspiration, instruction, or peace for you, you will hear Him when your soul is most at rest.

"Christ is killed in every generation, by those who have no imagination."

George Bernard Shaw

"The most notable impulse which I have ever experienced happened during a dream. Those who know Holy Scriptures will verify that there have always been warning and miraculous dreams, which either prophesy or direct the future, apparently as communications from heaven. And those people who have wandered into the history of God's people well know that God has not restricted this communication with Him to any particular time period."[2]

Taken from:
Dreams A Way To Listen to God
Morton T. Kelsey

2.   Morton T. Kelsey, *Dreams a Way to Listen to God*. (New York, N.Y: Paulist Press, 1978), p. 11.

"I shall know why—when time is over
And I have ceased to wonder why
Christ will explain each separate anguish
In the fair schoolroom of the sky.

He will tell me what 'Peter' promised
and I—for wonder at his woe—
I shall forget the drop to anguish
That scalds me now—that scalds me now!"[3]

Emily Dickinson

3.   Thomas H. Johnson, ed. *The Complete Poems of Emily Dickinson.* (Boston, MA: Little, Brown & Co., 1960), p. 91.

The Battle Hymn of the Republic

"Mine eyes have seen the glory of the coming of the Lord
He is trampling out the vintage where the grapes of wrath
are stored
He has loosed the fateful lightening of his terrible swift
sword
His truth is marching on.

Glory, Glory Hallelujah
Glory, Glory Hallelujah
Glory, Glory Hallelujah
His truth is marching on.

In the beauty of the lilies Christ was borne across the sea
With a glory in His bosom that transfigures you and me
As He died to make men holy, let us die to make men free
While God is marching on.

Glory, Glory Hallelujah
Glory, Glory Hallelujah
Glory, Glory Hallelujah
His truth is marching on."

Julia Ward Howe
© 1862
Stanzas I,V

Chapter 10

The Footsteps
of the Lord

"I am silver and exact. I have no preconceptions. Whatever I see I swallow immediately just as it is, unmisted by move or dislike. I am not cruel, only truthful.

The eye of a little god, four cornered."[1]

"Mirrors"
Sylvia Plath

1.   Sylvia Plath, *The Collected Poems.* (New York, N.Y: Harper & Row Publishing, 1981).

Recent studies suggested that by the year 2000 thirty-one countries will be able to produce nuclear weapons. I wonder if we will see the year 2000. I wonder if the world has that much time, till Christ returns. Listen to what a medical doctor has to say about the threat of nuclear armory. His report was recently published in a national magazine.

"We know from the effects of the detonation of a single bomb over Hiroshima that hundreds of people would be seriously burned. It amazes me to learn that all the medical resources of the United States, the richest country in the world, could not cope with even a few hundred burn victims at one time. I cannot imagine what people have in mind when they say that a strong civil defense would improve our chances of surviving a nuclear war. Most doctors, nurses, and technicians would be killed in an attack. Hospitals would be destroyed. So there would be few left with enough knowledge and equipment to save anybody."

As bishops recently have stated in the response to the arms race, "The moral issue at stake in nuclear war involves the meaning of sin in its most graphic dimension." When the world is spending $550 billion in arms (twice as much as it spends on food), you have to wonder if the "unthinkable" could happen in this generation. A nuclear war, which could destroy 800 million in a few hours, can be launched on the decision of a single man. Knowing this, anyone who doesn't pray for world leaders is extremely foolish. Read First Timothy 2:1-4 if you doubt that we, as citizens, have a moral responsibility to pray for men in government. I recently read an article about a pair of doctors who saved some 8,000

Polish people from death in a Nazi labor camp by spreading a so-called "typhus epidemic." Nazi officials, back in 1942, were fearful of that contagious disease being spread, and so avoided the area and its residents. What is not printed, however, and what is not often found in the front headlines, is the thousands of prayers that must have been sent to God from Poland, to have God intercede in so clever and powerful a way.

If you want the truth, it was the "prayers and supplications" of faithful believers that ended many a war, that saved many a soldier, and intervened in war-time strategy. The Bible (especially the Old Testament) is laden with results of how God interceded in behalf of His people. From the time of Moses to the days of Daniel up to this present day, God always intercedes for those who trust Him.

We are not defeated, and neither is a country that remembers her God. Our God's arm is not too short to save, nor, is He deaf to a plea from a people. It is precisely in the threat of total obliteration from this earthly home that we shall see how powerful our God is. God is not mocked.

"And God said / Prophesy to the wind, to the wind only for only / the wind will listen."

"Ash-Wednesday"
T. S. Eliot

Chapter 11

The Choice

Prometheus

Forms more real than living man,
Nurslings of immortality![1]

Taken from:
Prometheus Unbound Act I, 1.748
Percy Bysshe Shelly

---

1. Percy Bysshe Shelley, *Prometheus Unbound Act I, 1.748*, Wallace
    A. Briggs, ed., *Great Poems of the English Language*. (New York,
    N.Y: Tudor Publishing Company, 1936), p. 524.

In Greek religion, the Titan god Prometheus gave fire and the arts to men. This angered Zeus, who sent the vultures down to devour Prometheus' liver and set to destroy him. Zeus was angered at the god who loved mere men that much, so much, that he equated himself with them. Might and violence fought to destroy man, yet always because of knowledge and wisdom (that can't be taken away) did Prometheus yield himself to man for the continuation of man. He gave his most celebrated gift: practical reason. As Prometheus is chained against the craggy rock and preyed upon by vultures, he did it all because he stooped to help man.

I wondered whose hand guided Aeschylus' hand, in what he could not yet see.

"I knew when I transgressed nor will deny it
In helping man I brought my trouble on me
but yet I did not think that with such tortures
I should be wasted on these airy cliffs."

Prometheus Bound
Aeschylus

If you can't see the connection here, you will never understand the sages.

"Faith"

It was mercy that nailed Jesus to the cross. God's mercy for us, poured out in love, through Christ.

I solemnly assure you, said Jesus, "The man who hears my word and has faith in Him who sent me possesses eternal life."

John 5:24 NAB

The man who believes in it and accepts baptism will be saved; the man who refuses to believe in it will be condemned.

Mark 16:16 NAB

Yes, God so loved the world that he gave his only Son, that whomever believes in him may not die, but have eternal life.

John 3:16 NAB

I repeat, it is owing to his favor that salvation is yours through faith. This is not your own doing, it is God's gift.

Ephesians 2:8 NAB

"Sanctified Life"

Not everyone who says to me "Lord, Lord," will enter into the Kingdom of heaven, but only he who does the will of my Father in heaven."

Matthew 7:21 NIV

The Son of Man will come with His Father's glory accompanied by His angels. When He does, He will repay each man according to his conduct."

Matthew 16:27 NIV

Do you not know that God's kindness is an invitation to you to repent? In spite of this, your hard and impenitent heart is storing up retribution for that day of wrath when the just judgment of God will be revealed, when the will repay every man for what he has done: eternal life for those who strive for glory, honor, and immortality by patiently doing right; wrath for those who selfishly disobey the truth and obey wickedness.

Romans 2:4-8 NIV

In Greek mythology, a generation was cursed with unbelief because of Cassandra. In reality, God tells us He will close mans ears to hear and their eyes to see, if men continue to rebel and not listen.

> *And if anyone tells you, "This is the Messiah," or "That one is," don't pay any attention. For there will be many false messiah's and false prophets who would do wonderful miracles that would deceive, even if possible. God's own children. Take care. I have warned you.*
>
> Mark 13:21 NIV

> *After the tribulation ends, then the sun will grow dim, and the moon will not shine, and the stars will fall out of the skies, and the heavenly hosts will be shaken. Then men will see the Son of Man coming in the clouds with great power and glory.*
>
> Mark 24:26 NIV

"Watch"

Matthew 24:36-51. Matthew 24:4-35. Mark 13. Luke 21.

Genesis 3 shows us that it was disobedience that interrupted God's plan to unite us with Himself in everlasting life. Jesus Christ was sent, by the Father, that this plan might continue.

Matthew 22:1-14. Matthew 25:1-13. Luke 14:16-24. Matthew 13:24-30 NIV.

Heaven is real.

So is hell. READ ON.

Matthew 22:13. Matthew 24:51. Matthew 25:30. Matthew 3:12. Matthew 13:30. Luke 3:17. Mark 9:48. Matthew 18:9. Mark 9:46,47. Matthew 18:7-9. Luke 16:19-31. Matthew 7:13-14. Matthew 24:40-41. Matthew 25:30. Luke 16:28. Romans 2:8 NIV. This is all for starters. Get a taste of God. Heaven and hell do exist; Jesus only tells the truth. Jesus is truth.

"His Return"

Daniel 7:13. Matthew 25:31-46. Mark 13:26-27. Acts 1:11. 1 Corinthians 15:22-23. 1 Thessalonians 4:6-17. 2 Timothy 4:8. James 5:7-9. 1 Thessalonians 5:2. 2 Peter 3:10.

For as lightning comes from the east and shines as far as the West, so will be the coming of the Son of Man.
Matthew 24:27 NIV

Do not be like the Faustus who did not listen to the good angel on his left saying "Turn to God." Listen and live.

Journeys Ended, Journeys Begun

"Journeys ended, journeys begun: to go where we have never been, to be beyond our past, moments of lifting up, transcending death, rising in transparent light the fullness of God's presence. Alleluia, Alleluia, Alleluia."[2]

Taken from:
Journeys Ended, Journeys Begun
Songs of Weston Priory

---

2. The Monks of Weston Priory, *Songs of Weston Priory*. (Weston Priory Productions, Weston, Vermont 05161).

Chapter 12

Creation's High Notes

The Diamond

Physically and spiritually, all of life is an ebb and a flow, a shifting of the sands, a shaking of the grains. All of life is a seed and an egg, a germinated seed that grows to even stronger life than the one it came from. Even the harsh winds that blow in the scorching sun produces fruit 100 times more plentiful than that which was originally burned by the heat. Every principle of perfection begins with a grain of sand rubbing against a softer surface to produce a dazzling glow. The toughest metals and minerals that *have not been removed* through the seasons of time, are the elements that have been honed through this process: it is as this with the sons of God. Is there ever any real growth without pain? I have learned pain and joy are as married as the sun and moon. Father moon cloaks his earth by night to watch and brood over the house of earth while his children sleep, and his wife, the sun smiles at the morning and spreads out her skirt to blanket the earth in warmth and to nurture her sons to grow and bud and play in the noonday sun. All of life is a season: an ebbing, a toiling, a tearing, a stretching, a growing, a living, and a dying.

The great beauty of God is that He has made a cavernous deep in the season of man's soul that no stretching will rip, no sun can scorch, and no moon can hide. They "shine like the stars in the firmament" and will last forever because they are children of the diamond of the universe.

Our God has Himself been cut for us. He is the diamond of the universe.

"Love, like Death,
Levels all ranks, and lays the shepherd's crook
Beside the scepter."[1]

The Lady of Lyons
Act IV, Scene 1
Edward Bulwer–Lytton

---

1.   Edward Bulwer–Lytton, *The Lady of Lyons*, Act IV, Scene 1, c.
      1828, ch.33, Bartlett's Familiar Quotations, p. 601.

The Observing Mind

The wisdom and stature of God the Father was fully in Jesus. No wonder He was a man well-acquainted with sorrows. One can be brimming to overflow with joy and zest yet still be shaken with sorrows, if one knows or understands too much.

Ecclesiastes 1:18 says it best "For in much wisdom is much grief: and he that increaseth knowledge increaseth sorrow."

I have prayed for wisdom since I was born again but glad my soul that I know the 'joy of the Lord is my strength.' How grateful I am He gave me an exceedingly joyful heart. Were it not for joy (even for a sense of humor), I could not have lasted, for understanding rips the heart in two.

"People are forever asking me where I get my ideas, but one has only to listen, to look, and to live with awareness. As I have said in several of my stories, all men look, but so few can see. It is all there, waiting for any passerby."

Taken from:
Louis L'Amour, *The Education of a Wandering Man,* p. 29

The Prophetic Power of Faith

When Jesus told His own *don't throw what is holy to the dogs*, He was not being unkind. Understand what He meant. Would you throw your mink coat down on the floor to use as a throw rug? Would you give a two-year-old real money to play with and color on? Jesus was saying nothing is more important than our faith in Him, trust in God, and the willingness to believe **all** that He said to us.

God reveals the "mysteries of the Kingdom" by the Spirit, to those who believe in the Alpha and the Omega: the God of yesterday, today, and tomorrow. He does not change. Even to *believe* these words requires faith, and the carnal mind (the mind of human reasoning) does not yet possess the faith to see beyond the four corners of its own understanding.

God does not share His gifts with those who trample them, mock them, and call them nonsense. This is why when Jesus asked the disciples, "Who do you say that I am?", and Peter said "Thou art the Christ, the Son of the living God," Jesus smiled and said, "Peter, flesh and blood (carnal reasoning) did not reveal this to you, but my Father which art in Heaven." Only by faith can we comprehend even the mysteries of Creation!

P.S.: God did not use a road map to invent the universe or us…He spoke and out of the fire of His mouth it was created (the real "Big Bang" was not a theory)!

Many are the times when God prepares His beloved (those who trust Him) for that which is about to happen (change, sudden blessing or loss, testing, events which could unsettle one's faith). The Lord prepares us by speaking to our hearts. His holy gifts [words of knowledge, words of wisdom, prophetic utterance, the heavenly prayer language, and others. See Rom. 12:6; 1 Cor. 14:1; 2 Cor. 9:9; Eph. 4:8; Heb. 2:4] are for the building up of His Church. Many dear children of God have been duped into believing that the gifts of the Holy Spirit were done away with at Pentecost: don't buy that lie. Until we are with the Lord, we ain't ready! These gifts are to make us able to hear Him, move in His power, and reach the world for Christ. Now tell me, does the world look like it needs a touch from God? God no more stopped giving gifts to His Church than you stopped feeding your children meals because that was for then, not now. Truly the prophet prophesied God's thoughts when he said, "My people perish for lack of knowledge."

How often in everyday life, even the place of business, you can sense God's love for people, you can know God's calling on their lives, and know from experience that unless the Lord has planted that seed of faith in their hearts, or they are open to God, they will reject the love of God. Kind of like "kill the messenger", 20th century style. Unless someone is open to the Spirit of God, they won't receive the One who sent them. Strange thing is that we are so close to the Son of God revealing His glory, judging with righteous judgments, completing all things in Him; and most folks are so busy with the cares of this world, they will miss the wedding feast. Matthew 25 is our invitation to be ready at Christ's return.

If those in the world need smarts for success, how much more do those who fight on their knees for the souls of men and nations? Had Daniel acted out of fear or impulsiveness, he would have reacted instead of acting in faith. Chances are if his heart was not at peace, he wouldn't have heard the Lord's voice, "I will deliver you." Had Esther had a fit when old Haman tried to kill her and all the Jews, pandemonium would have resulted and sure death. Because she trusted in her God to save her, He did.

Is it any wonder the Psalms talk of trust? David, the author, ran for his life over 20 times from insecure Saul, who tried to kill him, and David had done no wrong to him. But because he ran when God said "go," and waited when God said "be still," it was Saul who chased himself into oblivion. How do we hear His voice? It's a daily walk; He says He "rewards those who seek Him," and He does. If you speak God's ways to an unbelieving heart, your faith becomes food for jackals. If you think people in the public eye have great emotional roller-coaster rides (great highs and lows), just guess at how Elijah felt when he saw God answer so visibly, or Moses as he saw the Red Sea open. Our adversary sends fiery darts to crush hope and oppress the saints (all who believe in Christ) to try to put out their faith and stop their zeal for God. Yet, the risk to follow God is that this is part of the anointing. Ol' slewfoot knew he couldn't kill the Son of God and could have cared less how many prayer meetings he had, or how often he thought of God; but all hell broke loose when Jesus announced, "The Kingdom of God is at hand."

The reason satan wanted Jesus out of the picture is because *the anointing breaks every yoke*. It is in His Word! Satan doesn't care if there are 12 churches on every block, if you go to two prayer meetings a week, if Aunt Bessie bakes cookies for Sunday School, if three uncles are priests, or if your kids play angels in "The Bells of St. Mary's," it's no threat to him. What the adversary does fight is those who move in the power of Jesus Christ because it was Christ who kicked satan out of heaven. Remember Christ prophesying through Job, "I saw satan fall like lightning from the sky," and it was the Spirit of God who said to Eve, "Thy seed (from human lineage) shall crush the serpent's head!" To sum up, this is the hour of history when Jesus will restore all which was lost in the garden: mankind's royal priesthood, authority, divinity—Christ's nature in man—all that was robbed in the garden. And He does it through His Church: all who believe in the Son of God and move by His Spirit.

In just two short weeks, Mr. Handel, the great composer, anointed by the Holy Spirit, wrote "The Messiah." Two weeks! The anointing of God shows us what we lost when we decided to do it our way and work "by the sweat of our brow" (read Genesis). He penned, "the kingdoms of the world, have become, the Kingdom of our Lord, and of His Christ." And He (the Lord) shall reign forever and ever. Not just in heaven, but here on earth (see Lk. 11:2). Kingdom authority. Jesus Christ rose from the dead and called satan a liar! God is for man, even when we sinned against Him. No one loves us like Him.

"The Promised Land always lies on the other side of a wilderness."[2]

Havelock Ellis

Is it any wonder why the adversary attacks the Word of God? The enemy can deceive hearts (God calls it wickedness) into robbing themselves and their generation of the answer to life. It happened to Adam and Eve and every generation since. Jesus said, "You kill the prophets, then make statues to them." The father of lies, our adversary, attempts to work his deception and lies on every society, even in the highest court rooms in the land. The laws of society may say that the unborn are not living souls, yet murder in the womb has robbed this generation of tomorrow's doctors and teachers and thinkers. No wonder Jesus said "that the spirit of death was already in the world." (See First John.)

Think of the Jonas Salks, the Einsteins, the Elie Wiesels, and the Fiedlers, the great gifts of life that came to mankind because of God's prophetic blessing. No wonder the enemy tried to kill the Jews! The anointing is in the blessing! No wonder God told us to "choose life, not death".

Remember, God told Abraham, "all the nations [includes billions of souls] would be blessed because of one man's faith." Mary, the mother of Jesus, "pondered these things [the prophetic promises of God] in her heart." God alone is true and keeps His covenant. No one can swear on His name and cause things to come to pass but God, and no one has a

2.   Havelock Ellis, *The Dance of Life*, Bartlett's Familiar Quotations, p. 851.

name that upholds the heavens, but the Lord. No one has perfect integrity, for man's truth is always partly flawed. Yet Jesus in a man's heart is perfection.

The costly anointing is not without risk. God does not hand over the keys to the kingdom without faith in the Son of God. Before demons were cast out, the blind made to see, and the lepers healed, those who named the name of Christ were called loonies, fools, losers, and everything else in the book. Jesus made it clear: the cost to following the King (and inheriting the reward of being His own) is to risk your reputation, and any other test that might be put to you.

Jacob was tested in the area that was his closest desire: the beautiful Rachel he wanted to wed. Abraham was asked to sacrifice his only son in his old age. Did God not honor their faith with more than they could have imagined? Remember, He said, "Eye hath not seen, and ear hath not heard what He has prepared for those who love Him." All the prophets knew more tears than the Dead Sea, and be assured, the prophets did not die out with Malachi. Jesus Christ, who is a Priest, Prophet, and King forever, (see Heb. 4:5-6,14) the Living God Himself, has a royal household of believers around the globe.

We are more than conquerors. The apostle Paul had a life that was more than most could have handled: he suffered for the gospel's sake, yet the power of the love of God in His life could not be denied. With all this world can throw at the Church, those who know God (in spirit and in truth) would not trade the anointing of His presence for anything.

We are so close to seeing the return of the Lord Jesus Christ! Yet first, His Word states, we will experience one last great outpouring of His Holy Spirit, before...well, read the words of Jesus and the Book of Revelation, you'll catch the drift. Very soon, millions of people are about to have their names written in heaven's Book of Life; they will know the Lord and be born into an eternal destiny. Salvation is on its way.

Listen to what the Spirit of God is saying to the earth. The God who came to earth to serve, now the King of glory, is about to be honored in all the earth, and we all have been invited through the door of faith to have eternal life. Knowing Jesus Christ as Lord and being born into eternal life by His Spirit isn't an option, it is the only way into life and out of death (see Rev. 3:20). He stands at the door of our hearts knocking, and He has said that He alone is "the way, truth and life, no man comes to the Father but by Me." If you think any philosophy of good living and being a kind person and all that is going to take you to eternity, you have bought a lie as old as Eden.

As Jesus said, many false christs will come in His name (the Jim Joneses, Mohammeds, Buddhas, New Age gurus, and various assorted thousands of philosophies which abound), all which point to man for salvation. They point to self. Only the blood of God's own Son is the acceptable sacrifice to pay the price for our lives, and as the gospel succinctly says, narrow is the road that leads to life, and few be that find it. Broad is the way that leads to death.

Millions trust their mitzvahs (good works), grandma's prayers, "feel-good, I'm okay, you're okay, we're it" nonsense, or Christ consciousness theology (which uses "Christian" words but denies the necessity of believing in the salvation of the cross of the Lord Jesus Christ). Any psychology, theology, or idealogy which denies the cross, the death and resurrection of the Lord Jesus, all that He said and did, is from the pits of hell. It's not from God.

Look at what Jesus said, "if you believe in Me you'll have eternal life." There is no other Savior, and hell licks its chops waiting for those who die without believing in Calvary's cross. Trust God, there are no atheists in hell.

And yet God's message is a message of hope: He came to heal, save, and deliver, not to judge. Judgment is already in the world because of sin. Our names are written in death until He writes them in life. We just don't live a nice life, then check out and lay in a grave, that's it. We either go to be with the Lord or spiral downward at our last breath. God's Word pleads with people to come to Him because He wants "no man to perish," but to have eternal life, and a joyful one here too.

When all men stand before their Maker on that great day, His Word shows that many will realize the truth of the statement, "But Lord, when did we see you on earth, when were you in our midst?" A man or woman who is open will know, by the witness of the Holy Spirit who lives within, when they are with a believer. You can fast (as Jesus called us to fast for righteousness' sake) and still be more full, in fact brimming with His life, than with any food (worldly way of figuring things out) the world wants you to buy.

Choose the "bread of life" and the food that God gives. "Those who eat My flesh [His Words!] and drink My blood [believing in His atonement at Calvary's cross] have life in them." When you feast on His living words, they change you from the inside out. The communion that Adam and Eve shared before the fall was a wholeness and a glory we cannot comprehend. When sin entered the garden (a prototype of our souls, for we are the land or "earth" that God dwells in), man lost his communion, oneness, covering, and ate death when he ate his own ways (sin) instead of the glory God offered.

God says His words are spirit and truth because if you do not understand what He meant, you cannot know Him. When you are born-again and baptized in the Holy Spirit, He reveals Himself to you. Just like a foreigner cannot understand the language in a strange land, the Word of God says when we come to God (in our hearts) we are citizens of a new country: eternity with God and the generations that love Him. How can you speak the language unless you live there? How can you know God's voice unless you "sup" with Him? Those words sound familiar? The "Last Supper" was our invitation to enter His Kingdom and eat from the tree of life that He is.

If you think your life is over when you die, you are mistaken. You might have been "made in America," but if you want to spend "eternity in Heaven," the time to get your passport is now!

There are many things God shows those who walk by faith, and not by sight, that those who do not know God's voice cannot see. For instance, when Mary was visited by the angel Gabriel who announced the glorious event that was to happen to her, could she have called up the "Jerusalem Gazette" and shared the happy tidings? We both know the answer. They would have locked her up. Yet God gave her the wisdom to "ponder these things in her heart," and trust in God to deliver. Is it any wonder that those who answer the call of God in their lives must suffer for the Kingdom's sake?

Joseph, Jacob's son sold into slavery by his own brothers, is an example of God's fruitfulness in a place of affliction. The story of Daniel is a testimony to what courage in the face of death can do. Whether it is patriotism (the book of Esther and Deborah's story), longsuffering in order to obey (the book of Hosea), or loss before blessing (Jacob whose name was changed to Israel), God is the answer. There is no one alive today who cannot identify with someone in the Word of God, and God always makes a way to stand.

Through Much Tribulation Do You Enter the Kingdom of God

Through tears, searchings, testing, and trials are we brought past the veil from death to life. The cross has four points: death and victory, sorrow and joy. Just as the glory cloud that led the children of Israel from the wilderness to the promised land was a cloud by day, it was also a fire by night. On the side of obedience, the cloud speaks of the glory, power and presence of God. On the side of disobedience, the cloud speaks of the judgment, dealings and government of God. For a believer in Jesus Christ, the cross speaks of the trials and testings of our wilderness that we must endure (faith walk) as we learn about our God and His ways. It also speaks of His glory and presence in our lives. The promised land, (place of destiny, provision, blessing that God has ordained for our lives), is for those who overcome (Revelation), those who by faith "endured," by the Word of their testimony, by the Blood of the Lamb.

Consider John, the Baptizer.

Through much tribulation was he brought to the point where he would preach, "Repent, for the Kingdom of God is at hand." There was not much about him that made him look much different from anyone else. Yet his family knew he was different from his very birth. The birth of the baptizer of Jesus Christ was a miracle. His mother Elizabeth ("Oath of God, Consecrated to God") knew that he was the answer to prayer. That which is birthed from travail and deep groaning unto God brings with it the season for God to show His glory.

The *manchild* which is spoken of in the Book of Revelation is always birthed in a season of testing. In every generation, the *kingdoms of this world* try to hinder the voice of the Lord from coming forth, and as Jesus said, "with man it is impossible, with God nothing is impossible."

Consider Joseph, the son born to Jacob and Rachel, or Samuel, the son born to Hannah and her husband; the tears from these mothers produced a fertile womb for God to perform His purpose and plans for a generation that would need it.

Consider Jesus, the Son of God.

The beginning of every move of God is laden with the seemingly ordinary. It says of Jesus that there was nothing about Him which caused us to look at Him. He wasn't known because of His popularity with well-known causes nor celebrated because He was promoting Himself, because He was schooled in the finest synagogues of the day. He had a hidden life, a rather obscure existence. It was not by chance that the Scriptures reveal little of Him before His thirteenth birthday. He became who He was in God by being "hidden," as the Psalms said, in the cleft of the Father's hands.

True religion isn't born in public, it is borne in a private and inner life of righteousness. A secret, driven soul hungry for God and thirsty for life can only be filled by God.

Saints are ordinary people who are made noble not because of their goodness, but because they have yielded their need for life to God. Saints are made in secret, and to everyone who is sanctified by the cross of Calvary, you are thatsaint.

The Lord Jesus walked perfectly because the ministry in Him was pure grace and wisdom. Wisdom tests you by many fires, and grace sustains you through each one. Jesus was perfected on the back side of a desert to be brought before the courts of men that His own hands had made. The ultimate sacrifice for Jesus is that He was willing to die on a bed of nails with pain beyond all telling. Life may assign us different highways to travel on, yet we all need one certain comfort: the peace and grace of Jesus who assures us that "this is the way, walk ye in it."

Few recognized Jesus for who He was; indeed, those who knew Him closest said, *"did not our hearts burn within us when He spake?"* The Holy Spirit bore witness to Jesus' words, but they could not recognize Him since He appeared differently. The Lord often appears in a form not recognized by the flesh, and that is so no man can boast. Since those who know God "worship Him in spirit and truth," He reveals Himself to the soul who seeks Him with all his heart.

What John the Baptist learned about grace was taught by a rough land filled with locusts and wild honey. The fire (trials) often reduces the land to shrubs and locusts, but when the refreshing (grace) comes, the living again will taste like honey.

Consider Hosea.

They really thought the old man had flipped this time. "Stone her," said Miriam, the old widow down the street.

After all, the law says, "anyone caught in the act of adultery must die by stoning." They said to Hosea, "Can you really think you heard from YHWH? Have you not heard the teachings in the synagogues? She is unclean!!! Have nothing to do with her."

Hosea heard all these words. Over and over, so many times, he knew them better than they did. Little did they know that Hosea, alone in his sleep, would awake and cry out to God. Day in and day out, he cried out for mercy. He begged the God of Abraham, Isaac and Jacob, "Deliver her or remove her from my life. But please Father of Abraham, don't leave me like this." He had cried so hard his eye lids had become creased. His heart, long broken, would beat so loud it would wake him at night. Yet in the morning, when joy comes (Psalms), he would feel strong again, strangely renewed, and know that he would know what to do concerning his wife.

The hardest part of his test was who would believe that he had heard from the Lord? He sat alone at the synagogue these days. Who would sit with a man so strange? "He does not divorce his harlot wife, and worse yet, he mumbles something about this being God's test." "Can you believe this man's sayings?" an old Rabbi asked another after Sabbath sundown had passed. "He says this has to do with *our* people, he says something about this is what Jehovah-God says about us, His very own people. Why, the audacity to speak such a thing outside these temple walls. This is Jacob's land, does he not know that?" they asked.

Hosea could not have known that God would write the Bible, His love book for the Church, out of the lives of ordinary men, from the pages of the goodness of man and the sin of man. How could Hosea have known that God would use his misery (yet, his obedience) to tell the story of His own broken heart for the people of the Covenant?

He did not understand what the Messiah was to suffer, but one day, when he missed his wife terribly, he found himself begging God to bring her back. He would take her back, no matter what the people would say. And the Word of the Lord came to him that he was living out what God lived out in His heart, for his wife, those who believe in His name. The thought came to him that he must tell the Rabbis how he still loved his wife and would rather die in her place, that he cannot make himself unlove her. Imagine how the prophet Hosea must have felt when he obediently, at God's command, told the priests and the people in Israel of the grieving heart of God. Hosea was not a priest who lacked descriptive words to tell of God's grief at Israel's rebellion, the Lord was making certain his words were packed with truth. Hosea was chosen for the ignonimous role of living out a tough message: he was married to a very unfaithful spouse, a harlot. Mercifully, after many tears and many lovers, Gomar, Hosea's wife, comes back to her senses and returns to stay with her husband Hosea. What a lesson of love this is for the Church, and what a picture of the faithfulness of God.

How could Hosea have known he wouldn't have been alive to see this?

Years would pass. Children would be born. Gomar, his wife, would come into his life, just long enough to give him hope, then leave, breaking his spirit in grief. Yet in every day, beneath the tears, he was somehow at peace. He knew God would come through, and this is the only thing that kept him going.

At an old age, finally, Gomar was reconciled with Hosea.

America, like Israel, was a covenant-made land. Like Gomar, we need to come back to the Lord with a pure religion: faithfulness, mercy, and sincerity of heart.

Consider God's servant Job.

Only a miracle of God kept the walls of Job's faith from crashing in. In a short span of time, he had to learn how to endure senselessness, grief, and numbing sorrow the way one endures a hurricane: you brace yourself against a strong shelter.

Until the day of his infamous misery, spearheaded by the Almighty Himself, Job had loved his life and everything about it. He had it all: family, health, wealth, honor and a long life. Now, Job despaired even of life. All that love has meant to him became the antithesis of all he scorned. Until a drastic parallel is raised in our own lives, we cannot comprehend others sorrow *in the heart*.

The strong emotion of grief became the welcome respite of numbness, and Job got to the point that he waited to die. A company of ne'er-do-well friends had only exacerbated Job's torment, for instead of water, he was given bitter herb for his "why's." He could not, as his wife suggested, curse God and die. Job still (in spite of God who tore down my house and plowed my children like wheat, he thought) loved Him, and most of all, he knew that He was God. The days seemed like years, and Job's not-to-comforting mate took temporary shelter in the next town, refusing to be a part in the questions and waiting on a God who could do such a thing. At first, Job missed her, then he realized his place was on the heap, with oozing sores and rotting skin guaranteed to make his wife more miserable than she already was.

After every friend—man, woman, and child—walked by and left, taking with them their own critique of the tragedy, Job was alone with God. The silence became more of a friend than enemy, and he welcomed the night. The day was too excruciating, for sight reminded him of his former life. Darkness promised nothing and asked nothing.

Lamentations to God became his antiseptic for his broken soul, and he welcomed the exhaustion that completed grief brought, at least he might get some sleep. At night he would dream of his children and see their beautiful faces filled with laughter. This was the most peaceful part of his life now, the memories that brought him joy.

Well, you know the end of the story. After his long mono-logue to the Lord, the Lord answered him, in a way he did not expect. God is rich in mercy and knows we are but flesh. He lavished blessings upon Job and his wife, giving him three beautiful daughters, and seven sons, which speaks of restoration and completion. After the fire, the most beautiful remnant of faith is what God gives as an offering.

Funny thing, God spoke to Job about *who He was*; He did not give into Job's insistence for why He did what He did. God dealt with Moses in a similar fashion. It seems that the Lord wants His people to know who the *I AM* is, not *why* the *I AM* does what He does.

Perhaps, not until heaven, was Job aware of the great testimony of faith he was to God in the sight of the mocking lucifer, who dared God and insisted that he could get any man to curse God to His face. God knew what Job was made of. I wouldn't be surprised if Jesus and Job stand side by side, victorious, looking out of heaven's glory, knowing that the adversary is still frustrated by Job, centuries later, because of his testing in God.

Folklore has it that the heavenly angels were so moved by what they saw Job endure that day that they asked the Lord if they could come to the earth that day and cry this man's tears, so he wouldn't have to. Scripture tells us that the angels long to peer into the things of salvation. From that day on, the angels had pity on all of Job's children, and the children of this man cried no more tears from that day forward because God sent Job angels to kiss his face whenever he remembered his loss—and he could not remember anything but joy.

And, remember Jacob?

Jacob learned to walk with his limp. After his encounter with God at Gilgal, he would always be left with a physical reminder of his battle of faith, where he wrestled all night. Jacob's limp teaches us that when God has a plan and purpose for our lives, He will sometimes bruise us (in the battle where the Holy Spirit fights our flesh) to teach us a lesson we could not otherwise learn. He bruises us to heal us (and the Scriptures tell us that), and depending on the design and extent we will be used of Him, He (the Spirit of God) will fight the man (Jacob) in all of us, to make the earthen vessel clay that can contain more than just ourselves.

And these are just a few of the great company of believers whose lives have paved the way for the journey we must make. The company of saints looks over heaven, even now, and cheers for us to win our race with the sweet rewards given for faith. They remember us, the seed that was left by faith.

...And the Lion Will Lie Down With the Lamb

Visionaries and agriculturists are deadbolts in the hand of God. They have the vision and foresight to lock out the intruder of time and greed that would plunder the land for a spoil. Usually, not welcome in their own generation, they are seen as a threat to modernization, but the generations that follow recognize them as visionaries and missionaries to the good earth. Guarding and preserving the land for the future is not an unholy thing. There is a wonderful park where I often walk, where it is not uncommon for hundreds upon hundreds of ducks to come from their pond and near your hand, look for a snack. Squirrels, very familiar with the humans with peanuts in hand, are eager to arrest your attention. They sit right up in front of you and wait for a treat. I have never seen anything like it.

There is a park where ducks, squirrels, birds and precious living creatures have found a sanctuary and a home. It is as if Emerson's thoughts come alive, and it is not hard to feel the joy of life and her creatures that was in this man when he penned *On Walden's Pond.*

It is not unusual to stroll through this park any Saturday or Sunday and see every size, shape, age, and color of Americans enjoying this place. Young lovers kissing, young mothers with toddlers tugging at their legs, the senior set going hand-in-hand at dusk, it is a gracious feast for the eyes, if you believe in life.

As I opened my mouth to taste the brisk December air, the words from the book that is alive, came to mind, "...and the lion shall lie down with the lamb." We know that Scriptures refer to this time of peace (reign of Christ, the time of the government of God, the time which the feet of Jesus Christ come to David's throne, in the city of Jerusalem, and He reigns, in perfect government, upon the earth). If there were ever a time to be alive, a time to know God and His Christ, this is it! It will be a day of truth in the land, and a day when the King establishes His government and no man will usurp his authority. A day of mercy, and a day of truth. A day where the Scripture "mercy rejoiceth over judgment" will come to its fruition: sinners will be forgiven, as in a second of time, as on the cross. Yet the wicked (those with hatred in their heart toward Christ and His cross) will not go unpunished. Widows and the poor will have a fair day in court, and this government will not allow victims to lose and sinners to win. This day will expose, and it will correct. For those who love God, this is the day the great company of saints will love to see.

The lion and the lamb. Jesus came as a lamb, a defenseless baby; He was slaughtered as the atoning lamb for all mankind's sins (see Gen. 22:8-14; Jn. 1:29-30; Acts 8:32; Jn. 19:36; Is. 53). Revelation 5:5, Genesis 49:4, Isaiah 38:13 and Hosea 5:14 are just a few of the verses that remind us that *He is the Lion of Judah, the prophesied Redeemer and King.* He will roar as He rides the clouds to His throne. The next time the earth sees Jesus, they will "faint" and tremble, as did Paul, as did John on the Isle of Patmos. Those whose hope is in God in Christ Jesus have no need to fear.

The lamb will establish peace (mercy and kindness)...the lion will punish evildoers the Word tells us. Mercy mixed with righteous judgment, both the "mercy" and the "severity" of God (Romans 11:22). The balance of gentleness and discipline, royal authority and tenderness. This is what the earth has longed for since the beginning of time: balance. The lion and the lamb will bring perfection, wholeness, and completeness. It will all be done right.

One cannot mistake the presence of the law—the lion (in the Old Testament, it foreshadows the lamb to come—New Testament). The lion (the Ten Commandments) will lay down with the lamb (the blood). Righteous judgment lies down with mercy. Forgiveness is extended (from the Lamb) to all the sincere and contrite of heart (or those willing to live a life of repentance), but to stiff-necked and hardhearted (heart of stone), they will be cut off from the land of the living (the roar of the lion). It is impossible not to see all that God foreshadows, He fulfills.

The visionary, the prophet, the teacher, the rabbi, the agriculturist, the economist, the judge, the law-giver, the healer, the redeemer, the roar and authority of the Kingship of His mane, the protector and mercy of the healer. The lion and the lamb are one: He lay down on a cross to come to His throne.

"We should all be concerned about the Future because we will have to spend the rest of our lives there."[3]

Seed For Thought
Charles Franklin Kettering

---

3.   Charles Franklin Kettering, *Seed For Thought*, Bartlett's Quotaions, p. 940.

Sand-dial of the Sages

Time magazine's fall 1992 issue, *Beyond the Year 2000*, had some interesting glimpses about our past millennia, and the one that looms before us, the 21st century. It comes as little surprise to me that the magazine's "top ten" of notables, in millennia past, were names associated with a strong degree of faith. Invention, discovery, inventors and heroes, in my way of thinking, are part of the persona of men marked by their Creator to reflect the glory that lies in humanity.

St. Francis of Assisi's life reminded many of the beauty and simplicity of faith, the wonder in all God's creatures. Johann Gutenberg was an instrument of God to bring the gospel into the new world ("go ye into all the world and preach the good news"). After the dark ages, the good news was that liberty could be read: the printing press came to be. Columbus, the young lad Christopher, might have had personal ambitions, but after reading about this man's life, you'll never convince me he didn't feel "called" or "compelled" by a blueprint already written by the Master playwright, to sail off for a new land. And on, and on. Even the legendary Shakespeare exhibited writings that would inspire and intrigue many centuries later. How could a man write, "the quality of mercy is not strained, it falleth as the gentle dew from heaven," how could one say that, unless, one had tasted the necessity for mercy? A drop of mercy is life to a thirsty and weary soul. Nota bene my friend; brilliance, creativity, discovery, these do not happen by chance. We reflect the image of the Creator, and when wisdom, ingenuity, and courage are mixed with faith, the results are life-changing, altering the course of history.

For this reason, I have a healthy skepticism for those who look into the future without the safeguard of history as a valuable teacher. The Economic European Community won't bridge disunity any more than peace for the masses occurred when the census was taken that Caesar Augustus declared: it only accelerates man's rationale for absolute control (and the aftermath of WWI and WWII teach us such totalitarianism and economic and political control have devastating consequences).

Since man is not his own god, future generations would be aided far more if we could teach our children the most basic ingredient for any future: without God man is already dead. There is hope and life in Him, and alienation from the Creator results in anarchy against oneself, one's own species, and one's own planet.

2000 A.D. I hope I'm with those who believe in the One who wrote the Book of Revelation: the Creator Himself. Nothing is more dismal than to be with souls (who have not the hope of everlasting salvation within). Laughter is great, and it is a real blast to dance your merry soul with hope, but what cause is there to rejoice if your future is clouded with death?

> "Behold, I am coming soon! My reward is with me, and I will give to everyone according to what he has done. I am the Alpha and the Omega, the First and the Last, the Beginning and the End."
>
> Revelation 22:12-13 NIV

The Shout That Takes the World by Storm

Matthew's Gospel tells us that, "while the bridegroom tarried, they all slumbered and slept" (Mt. 25:5 NIV). The Lord takes His Church by surprise, and it seems for those who wait, His timing (the bridegroom, our Lord) often seems delayed for the things in our lives which we so eagerly await. Often times it seems God arrives on the scene through the back door, which is locked and seldom used. The Lord, who is always faithful, often uses the portals of entry in our lives that we would never use.

He comes in the night, meaning, when we can't visibly see His coming of His deliverance at hand. The custom of the Jewish wedding of long ago was such that the wedding celebration (which lasted a week) began with the bridegroom coming for his bride to snatch her away when the people were not looking. Then, the people would follow the bridegroom and bride to the place of festivities. No clearer analogy is needed. Jesus tells us what He intends: a deliverance of a bride, the consummation of a wedding, the feasting. The feast of tabernacles was celebrated in the Old Testament day; it will soon be celebrated by the Church in this time.

Those whose candles were not lit (light was needed to guide the way at night), could not go in. As we have heard, this is no time in history to be a foolish virgin, someone who doesn't have enough oil (Holy Spirit) in their lamp to carry them the whole way of the bridal journey.

Those who have lived in countries where suddenly their freedom to worship was taken are a lesson for us; you have to know the Lord for yourself, and enough life of God (in the Holy Spirit) has to be found to carry you through this life's journey. The times will come when it will seem like just you and God (and the closer the bridegroom gets, God will awaken [call] us , many times in the *night* of our journey, to see if we'll get out of slumber to watch and wait for His coming). There is a glorious day of His coming, yet even now, He is already here.

The Kingdom has already begun, and those who want life will always follow the light in the night.

Mercy Rejoiceth Over Judgment (James 2:13 NIV)

There is something about the appearance of one so tender and helpless that draws you into them. The presence of a small child invites mercy. To look at a child, we see the innocence in a state of perfection. A baby doesn't even know who or what it is: it only knows what it sees, and feels, and smells and tastes. The most basic senses, fully alive. It needs, but is not aware of the perception of need, it just needs to be held and loved and fed and changed. The lack of other-awareness is at its root "self", and the law of self or survival is there from birth; yet when consciousness has not marred the need, it has a beauty all its own. Some days I wonder if that is why hunters love to hunt and outdoorsmen commune with nature: even the animal kingdom reminds us of a lost innocence.

As I was watching the dedication of a baby at the morning service, I thought of Adam and Eve in the garden. The sense of protection and covering and joy and cherishing God the Father must have had in His heart when He looked at His son and daughter. In their untapped state of grace, they were no different in appearance than the small child that comes forth from the womb. For from the heart of God and the desire for a creation to fellowship with came His own. He begat a son, and from His son, he begat the wife. (Even as Jesus, the "first-fruit of righteousness," begat His wife, the bride).

The day came, when the consciousness of Adam and Eve was opened; the light was turned into dark, and death entered the garden (see Gen. 3:7).

As the man and his wife partook of the tree of knowledge, of good and evil, they did not know, these young children of God, that they were playing with fire that they were not prepared to handle. The glory of their outer garment was to be singed—and with it, their anointing. We can hardly comprehend what our first ancestors must have looked like, but the glory, oh my, the first children of God. When we sin (tell a fib, say unkind words, steal, lose our temper, whatever, you can look up all the deadly duos for yourself), there is a conviction, and it is a reminder of what we are. Cold reminds you that you need warmth—go get a covering (see Gen. 3:21); hunger reminds you to eat, lest you perish. Before the fall, there was no need to be reminded of anything. There was no conviction because there was no sin. A perfect love. A perfect union. Perfect joy. No frustrations. No fear. No disease. Nothing that marred the glory. The only way we can comprehend what we lost is to imagine every dream you've ever had, every hope for good, for truth, for beauty, for life, at its consummated state. The ideal!! In all things. This is what the perfect "Adam" came to earth for: to win back the innocence of relationship, the communion of fellowship with our Maker.

This is what happened when we (for we could not have done any differently than Adam and Eve) ate of the tree of death (mistrust of God, fear of God, doubt of God, disobedience of God). If you doubt this, wait till the adversary of your soul tempts you. You will realize you are naked without the cross. The temptations that are waged against us, and the inner struggles we war with in battling them, are evidence enough that we still are in need of deliverance from the world, the devil, and most of all, ourselves. Only a deliverance from this body of death can bring us into His glory. As Paul said, "lest I be a castaway, a reprobate, preaching something to you I don't face daily, let me boast that God loves a wretch like me: I am still being changed."

Imagine the baby you nursed at your breasts, bounced on your knee, held through the night, waking up one day, able to talk, and saying "I don't trust you mom and dad, I want my inheritance now. I know you're holding back on me—I want to be an adult like you, and know all that you know, NOW!" As bizarre as this seems, that is a picture of what happened when sin entered the world. When I get to heaven (by the power of His spirit and the blood He shed for me), I hope I have the privilege of meeting the real "first lady" and "first man." The human race owes them an apology. We wouldn't have done any differently because we (human nature) have not changed. The temptation in the garden (the devil didn't come with horns and ugly face), the "apple," was probably as seductive an interest as any of the distractions that are here today (false religions, new gurus, false Christs, "other gospels," all the entertainment that caters to the flesh).

That same serpent who deceived the first family, back in the garden of Eden, is still trying to pass off rotten fruit as good food. It may have been an apple, it can just as well be anything that looks very appetizing to the lust of the eyes, if the devil is handing out food, you know it is dead. No life can come from a lie. The adversary to man's soul always tries to counterfeit the real gift that God wants to give. There are many counterfeit doctrines today that promise everything without repentance, but they are just rotting lies. Just as the seed is always in the apple, the life of Jesus will only be in those with living fruit. Anything that offers life without the gospel is only death and destruction: "there is way that seemeth right to a man, but in the end leads to destruction" and "broad is the road that leads to destruction" (Mt. 7:13). One only has to look at all the "false christs" that are in the world today. As the Word says, the spirit of the antichrist is in the world at work today (New Age; Hinduism; Buddhism; religious "churches" with no life, that hinder or resist the anointing of the risen Christ; the modern mecca of sciences and arts that preach, "another gospel").

Thank God for Jesus. Thank God for the cross of Calvary. As the servant Paul said, "let anyone who preaches another gospel...he is already cursed." When our ancestors ate of the forbidden fruit, it opened their eyes to see a reality they were not ready for. When we eat of the fruit of knowledge, apart from the tree of life (the life of God in Christ Jesus), we partake of the emptiness of sin. You would never think of handing over your car keys and telling your five-year-old to take your car for a spin; only time will give him the maturity, strength, and knowledge to operate such a vehicle. In the fullness of time, I believe the Lord more than wanted to reveal much to His brand new, fresh from the womb of heaven, just born fruits: the man and the woman. Yet in their innocent state of grace, they could never handle the reality of what sin was, how it would destroy them and the innocence of life they had. He gave them all they needed for eternal life: He gave them His word, His love, Himself. They had no reason not to trust their "Abba" daddy, but in the temptation, they believed the "lie" that God was holding back on them. Thank God that "mercy rejoiceth over judgment."

Chapter 13

A Voice in the Wilderness

Justification by Trust

The human mind is such a complex and marvelous machine. One common character among almost all minds is the need to validate (any) loss through redeeming the present. You know, the neighbor got a bum deal on a used car, and now he's trying to jack up the price to sell it to the guy down the street. He wants to justify loss through profit. A beautiful young bride remembers she was a fat little pudgy just years ago, and so she becomes anorexic in attempt to kill the image of imperfection. Our minds strive for harmony and order.

You know, I am learning that Jesus Christ is our justification. He validates our existence by virtue of our being. Past, present and future—all become one glance in God's view of His children.

Our lives are ultimately validated through what we believe, how we live what we believe, and what we strive for.

Heaven allows every man to create his own epitaph, forming his own legacy.

Make the pages of your life a well-read book. Salvation is destiny!

"When you are old and gray and full of sleep,
And nodding by the Fire, take down this book."[1]

Taken from:
When You Are Old
William Butler Yeats

---

1. William Butler Yeats, *When You Are Old*, *Bartlett's Quotations*, p. 879.

Put It in Writing!

We can all relate to this. You gave away great ideas, buried treasures, pieces of jewelry or contract proposals, but did not first put it in writing. How many promotions, commissions, promises, vows, and dreams go by the wayside because man takes verbal commitments less seriously than the written word.

Well, the first lawyer knew the heart of man better than man himself. Ever hear of Mt. Sinai, the Ten Commandments? Think the Lord doesn't understand the power of the written word? Legal defense began with a contract between the dirt and the wind, and the soul of man was written down in the Book of God. He put it in writing, sealed it shut with a blood covenant and blew the wind of His Spirit across generations who would read it! Talk about signed, sealed and delivered!

Did you know 'soul-food' can be holy? Ever hear of "converted rice?"

Jill's Perms

Last time Jill cut my hair and gave me a perm, I asked her if she had the "gift of the working of miracles." I mean, it doesn't hurt to ask, does it? I don't want to spend this year looking like mad for electric shock treatments.

What God Can't Do

Do you want to know what God can't do? He can't make you love Him. He can make a robot, but He can't force you to love Him. Who would want a forced love? Not I, would you?

In giving men the choice to accept or reject His love, God made Himself as vulnerable to us as we are to each other.

"O, time thou must untangle this, not I; It is too hard a knot for me to untie."

Twelfth Night
Act II, Scene II
William Shakespeare

The Mystery of X and Y

The Tablets of Law and Science tell us in creating them "male and female" God created us for fellowship and sonship in a symbiotic way.

Christ (the seed of Divine Love) is born to life wherever faith is born. Faith is birthed by the germinating seed of trust and hope.

Jesus must derive great pleasure in the union of two souls consumed in Him, and flowing in that continuity to each other. The mystery of "X" and "Y" is not alone in masterful genetic engineering, but is the genius of spiritual chemistry. If you've ever had the sense of time standing still, it's a refreshing moment where you are awed by the very ordinary passing of time—which somehow has taken on a rarified quality. In *that* moment, what a peace enters our hearts. Love is like this: what a glorious moment when X and Y find their place in YAHWEH. Math is complete because it is infinite, and in Christ there is no dimension of end. Remember, the end of (death of the egg when it unites with the sperm gives birth to the zygote, a new life. God designs life to spring forth even out of death; the resurrection process is alive in every part of life.

The Continuum of Life

I remember a protractor being the most interesting tool of geometry class. If you are quite careful, you wouldn't tell where the circle began and where it ended. How like life. Where does it begin? In a womb, in a dream, in the imagination of a Creator? Did it begin before sand was on the shore or billions of years before the stars were made; were you and I a hope in God, only to be revealed at a later place in time?

The shortest distance between two points is a straight line, and the shortest distance between heaven and earth is your prayer.

"I wake to sleep, and take my waking slow. I feel my fate in what I cannot fear. I learn by going where I have to go. We think by feeling. What is there to know? I hear my being dance from ear to ear. I wake to sleep, and take my waking slow."[2]

Taken from:
The Waking
Theodore Roethke

---

2.   Theodore Roethke, *The Waking, The Norton Anthology*, p. 2,267.

Rule of Thumb

I have a rule of thumb for gauging myself. On being the boss, would I want to work for me? Am I fair, supportive? Do I expect more of people than I want to give? Is my authority free of discriminations, prejudices, and narrow-thinking? In short, would I be eager to work for me?

Would I want to be married to me? Is it a pleasure or a pain? Is life delicious or has it lost its flavor? Is he eager to come home to me?

Ask yourself the same question if you are a parent, a priest, a rabbi, a child, a friend.

The answers may surprise you. Strive to become what you need most from others.

Acceptance, freedom and unconditional love is the paradise every living soul longs for. Strive to become like Christ.

Overheard Near the Waterfront 2,000 Years Ago

"Hey Peter, hurry up pokey, or you'll miss the boat."

Peter, with a grin, "No thanks, I'm walking home."

Chapter 14

Same Words,
Different Generations

Hamlet's famous soliloquy is not all that different from Solomon's woes in Ecclesiastes 1:2.

The all-too introspective Prince of Denmark should have heeded Solomon's advice about a good wife being a good thing. His own troubled soul forfeited him a life with Ophelia. Hamlet thought too much and lived too little.

Even the apostle James recognized the brevity of this life with its passing glories. (See Jas. 4:14.)

Eternity, like joy, is there for the taking. Live.

Can You Feel the Fire?

I know the psalmist was trying to describe the presence of the Lord he felt within him when he said, "The spirit of a man is the candle of the Lord." Have you felt the candle burning recently? (See Proverbs 20:27.)

Designer Genes

The Welcome Wagon Lady was telling me how her kids were commenting that all the kids at school had designer jeans except them. She felt a little apprehensive about her inability to provide much on one income.

Kids often have a limited focus between needs and wants. Kids from age five to 90, I guess.

I told Sue we all own designer jeans, anyway. I pointed to my nice-looking (discount) slacks and said, "See, here's the weave of Calvary." She laughed, and I thought how He truly has sewn the thread of His garment into our lives. We do wear the cloth of His righteousness. So who says you can't look nice on a disciple's salary, anyway?

When Christ "designed" you from His holy imagination, you had "designer genes" in your mother's womb. Before you were born, you were already rich.

A Shaft of Light

The look of an infant the first time he looks into his mother's eye, or is held by his father high in the air—this is the most powerful gospel the adult sees.

A shaft of the light of Christ is most clearly seen unencumbered by semantics or doctrines or litanies; it is best seen in eight pounds, seven ounces of truth staring back at your soul.

How can you resist so tender, the Savior?

"In the midst of winter, I finally learned there was in me an invincible summer."

Taken from:
Actuelles
Albert Camus
(1913-1960)

Wheat and Chaff

Your heart is a garden; you have to till it with care. You have to set the Word to your heart as a brushfire—a consuming fire that clears the land to purge it clean so only new growth can come forth.

Where There is Love...

Where there is no (true) mercy, there is little (true) revelation. Spiritual discernment is as closely linked to mercy as the weather is determined by atmospheric pressures. Unless understanding holds the hand of love, you have nothing more than a charlatan wearing the king's clothing.

The Tool of the Husbandman

Jesus sent the Holy Spirit into the world to convict the world of sin. As His Spirit convicts of sin, He also comforts the believer and gives him grace to change (repent).

When John the Baptist prophesied that the axe was laid at the root, he was speaking of the reign of the Kingdom of God, which was manifested in Christ Jesus.

The most sure sign that we walk with the Spirit of God is conviction of sin. The Holy Spirit (gently, yet most assuredly) convicts us where we do not look, talk, act or exhibit the grace of the One who saves us. When the axe is laid to the root of the tree (sons of men), all that is dead and not rooted in life (the true vine, Jesus) will be done away with. God gives us grace to change, not to resist change.

Remember when Jesus said to Peter, "Peter, who do you say that I am?" Peter answered by the revelation of the Holy Spirit. Jesus said that His Father in Heaven revealed His truth to Him. Jesus, the King of kings, defined what rank'n' file really is like: He washed His disciples' feet.

We need to know each other in spirit (that is, truth). The gospel promises the day will come when we will "know each other even as we will be known."

The Songstress Voice That Shakes Away the Clouds

The April clouds hang overhead like a bucket about to be tipped, but I am not shaken. I have my faith, my hope, my dreams, and His love to carry me through whatever storms cast their pall over my day. I think the gifts of faith and hope are given to us to borrow because we have not yet received eyes that look out into eternity. Faith and hope can carry us with mercy, not unlike a mother carries her child on her hip, if we are willing to rest being a child of faith.

I am feeling like music: not just to hear it, but to be it. I turn on the radio, and the songstress is singing. What a voice and what words! Her voice is like a storyteller's charm that draws you in. A great voice, a rich voice is not unlike one of the many colors of my God. Even a violinist with left fingers gliding across the strings can give you as much of a peak at heaven as anything can. Music, laughter, anything that teems with life, you can find the Holy Spirit there.

Is life the dream or the reality? Heaven, I imagine, is more reality than this present place, which is but a dream that mirrors the destiny of all those who hope and have faith.

Planet of the Humans

One night, unable to fall asleep, I turned on the television to a late night movie. "Planet of the Apes" was playing, and I thought, after 20 minutes of this, I'll be ready for some zzzzzzz's. The storyline was that the governor of this planet of humans wanted to destroy this one intelligent ape on the planet whose name was Caesar. Apes were slaves to humans.

Caesar had a position of authority over the human beings, so Caesar asks the governor, "Why?" The governor tells him that the apes at the most basic level represented the "dark side" of themselves (the humans). In wanting to eradicate the "lower or darker" side of themselves, the humans thought that destroying the apes would destroy the darkness.

I thought how like man to try and destroy darkness (sin) through reason and might. Intelligence and force never destroy the darkness, for darkness is pervasive in itself. Only the blood of Jesus Christ has the power to reveal light, which repels the darkness.

It is only a movie, but how this world searches for the heroes by trying to eradicate darkness through external means.

As history has shown, you can't annihilate a people and hope to rid a land of darkness; the darkness must first be consumed within yourself. The intelligence of man (without divine grace) will destroy itself. The flesh destroys itself, but the Spirit sustains both spirit and soul life. The flesh lacks perspective and wisdom. This is why it can never be satisfied. The flesh has an end in itself because it has no divine life to sustain itself.

You can take Darwin, but I'll take the Divine. I might have started out in life with only a tail, but my end is to wear a crown. I might have been as an ape (before grace), but I now have the fragrance of royalty. I am a daughter of the King of the universe by faith in the Prince of Peace. *There's hope Church—"And the woman shall crush the serpent's head."*

How's that for a happy ending?

Sweet dreams.

A Battering Ram

The ram that was caught in the thicket that Abraham used as a sacrifice instead of Isaac was placed there by God. Abraham represents faith, those who lay hold of God's acceptable sacrifice by faith. The ram was as the battering ram Himself, Jesus Christ, who was given as a perfect sacrifice. And Isaac represents the sons of men, who would live, and not die, because through their faith in Jesus Christ, the perfect blood sacrifice was made. Because of Abraham's faith in God, his son lived. We live and have eternal life because of the sacrifice of the ram, the lamb.

The "battering ram" that resisted sin and overcame the world gave His life as a lamb.

The Turtle and the Hare

The turtle won the race, not because he was quick but because he was steady. In spiritual matters, a steady, enduring faith plunders hell's gate with more lasting results than quickshot prayers that are once and done. Consistency outdistances speed, and lifetime faith is for those in it for the long haul. The turtle wins the race.

Suddenly to His Temple

Malachi 3:1-3

If you walk with the Lord you see there are times the King will come suddenly to His temple! There will be seasons of your life where there will be an urgency for prayer, an urgency for repentance, a desire to be one with God.

"If today you hear His voice, harden not your hearts," the Scripture says. (See Hebrews 3:7-8 NIV.)

Revelation 20:4

The writer of Hebrews knew that "man is appointed *once to die,* then the judgment." Reincarnation is the counterfeit of resurrection, and those who go speedballing faster than light into eternity, into hell, will find laughing demons and weeping souls awaiting them.

The Lord gave me the Scripture Ezekiel 33:6 years ago and if I have learned anything, we are accountable for what we know. I will tell you this, as a child at church I used to say a prayer every Sunday "because I dread the loss of heaven and the pains of hell."

What do you want? The eternity of loss called hell or the promise of joy called heaven? Choose life.